Copyright © Salt Media Ltd
Published by Salt Media Ltd

The right of Salt Media to be identified as the author of this work has been asserted by it in accordance with the Copyright, Designs and Patents Act 1988.

A catalogue record of the book is available from the British Library.

All rights reserved. No part of this publication may be reproduced, distributed, or transmitted in any form or by any means, including photocopying, recording, or other electronic or mechanical methods, without the prior written permission of the publisher, except in the case of brief quotations embodied in critical reviews and certain other non-commercial uses permitted by copyright law.
For permission requests, write to:
Salt Media, 5 Cross Street, Devon, EX31 1BA.

While every effort has been made to ensure the accuracy of the information in this publication, we cannot be held responsible for any errors or omissions and take no responsibility for the consequences of error or for any loss or damage suffered by users of any of the information published on any of these pages.

Salt Media, 5 Cross Street, Devon, EX31 1BA.
www.saltmedia.co.uk
Tel: 01271 859299.
Email: info@saltmedia.co.uk

Written, designed and produced by Marcus Chapman, Nick Cooper, Lucy Deasy, Nik Farkas, Claire Fegan, Catherine Jones, Kathryn Lewis, Tamsin Powell, Jo Rees and Chris Sheppard of Salt Media.

Cover image of dish by Michael Wignall at Gidleigh Park by David Griffin.

Previous spread: Trencherman's Guide member chefs and 2015 Trencherman's Awards winners who cooked at the 2016 Awards night at The Seafood Restaurant. Left to right: Stuart Pate, Amy Symonds, Stephane Delourme, Anton Piotrowski, Dan Miles and Gordon Jones. Photographed by Guy Harrop.

Big salute to South West photographers David Griffen and Guy Harrop who created many of the stunning images featured in this year's guide.

The Trencherman's Guide is supported by

FOREWORD

Jamie Oliver's Fifteen Cornwall **No. 105**

I'm thrilled to welcome you to the 24th edition of the Trencherman's Guide.

It's hard to believe that the South West's most prestigious dining guide will be a quarter of a century old next year.

With that in mind, it's especially pleasing to see lots of new and exciting additions this year.

To help you navigate your way through this exceptional group of restaurants, we've created a series of new Trencherman's Collections which detail fabulous experiences such as places to feast on seafood by the sea or indulge in an exquisite afternoon tea. You'll find the guide peppered with them.

In addition, Susy Atkins of BBC One's *Saturday Kitchen* explores the world of the sommelier in her feature on page 20.

You can get involved with the Trencherman's Guide through the fortnightly email newsletter which details great events, features and fabulous experiences – sign up at www.trenchermans-guide.com and follow on Facebook and Twitter @Trenchermans.

Enjoy the guide,

Jo Rees
Editor, food Insider's Guides

CONTENTS

Rock Salt Cafe **No. 67**

12	Welcome by Michael Caines
14	Join the club
16	Trencherman's takeovers
18	Trencherman's Awards 2016
20	The Sommelier: friend or foe?
24	Using the guide
26	Gloucestershire
32	Wiltshire
42	Bath and Bristol
52	Somerset
62	Dorset and Hampshire
70	Devon
96	Cornwall
128	Index

WELCOME

Get ready to discover some phenomenal dining experiences in this year's Trencherman's Guide.

The 24th edition showcases exceptional chefs and restaurants, such as two Michelin-starred Restaurant Nathan Outlaw and Michael Wignall's new offering at Gidleigh. But in addition, it's the insider's guide to very special dining pubs, hidden-gem hotel restaurants and more casual gourmet experiences. The element that links them all is quality.

Trencherman's celebrates exquisite, creative cooking and pitch perfect service, and it's what the guide has stood for since it was created by a small group of chefs 24 years ago. And we maintain the quality of the guide by only inviting restaurants that meet the strict scoring criteria.*

You'll find lots of new restaurants in this latest edition - a sign of the up-and-coming establishments and talented chefs who are making their mark in the South West and it's also why the region is forging ahead with its reputation for world-class dining.

I hope you discover some new special places to eat out and stay.

Wishing you wonderful foodie adventures,

Michael Caines MBE
Chairman of *The Trencherman's Guide* editorial board

*Restaurants are invited to be in the guide on the basis of consistently high ratings across a selection of top international publications including the *Michelin Guide*, the *Good Food Guide* and the *AA Restaurant Guide*.

JOIN THE CLUB

The Trencherman's Club is a great way to find out about exclusive offers, special events and news from restaurants in the guide.

It's free and you'll get a fortnightly e-newsletter, plus access to events and the chance to vote in the Trencherman's Awards.

Sign up now at

www.trenchermans-guide.com

Join the conversation at

The Trenchermans Guide   @trenchermans

TRENCHERMAN'S TAKEOVERS

If you want to find out what goes on behind the scenes in Trencherman's members' kitchens, you don't need to book yourself a chef's table, just follow Trencherman's on Twitter.

In addition to bringing you news, offers and hot-on-the-pass shots of dishes as they disappear out of the kitchen, we're also handing over the Twitter controls to our chefs in a series of takeovers this year.

So far, the following chefs have taken us behind the scenes at their restaurants:

John Hooker of The Cornish Arms in Tavistock, Paul Berry of The Swan at Bampton, Dez Turland of Saunton Sands Hotel in north Devon, Matthew Beardshall of Wild Garlic Restaurant in Nailsworth, Steve Pidgeon of The Arundell Arms in Lifton, Sam Moody of The Bath Priory, Gordon Jones of Menu Gordon Jones and Chris Cleghorn of The Olive Tree at The Queensberry in Bath.

Breakfast with a #Seaview @SauntonSandsHot is there a better way and place to start the day
Dez Turland

Inspiration for today's fish dish, brill with morels and sea fennel - although sea fennel tastes like my grandad's shed!
Gordon Jones

Just getting ready for dinner service @stevenpidgeon @TrayYellOw @TheArundellArms only two of us #lets do 100!
Steve Pidgeon

You can follow the rest of the series for yourself on Twitter @Trenchermans

Chefs (clockwise from top left): Dez Turland, Matthew Beardshall, Chris Cleghorn and Sam Moody.

The South West's finest chefs, foodies, hoteliers and industry insiders came together in November to discover who had won this year's Trencherman's Awards.

The guide's readers voted in their thousands to crown their favourite restaurants, dining pubs, chefs and more. Then the eagerly anticipated results were revealed at a glamorous dining event at Rick and Jill Stein's The Seafood Restaurant in Padstow, with last year's winners each cooking a course for guests and finalists.

Here's who took the top honours - find them throughout the guide.

WINNERS	RUNNERS UP
BEST CHEF 84 John Hooker, The Cornish Arms, Tavistock	25 Gordon Jones, Menu Gordon Jones, Bath 78 Tom Williams-Hawkes, The Salutation Inn, Topsham
BEST RESTAURANT 120 Ben's Cornish Kitchen, Marazion	5 Wild Garlic Restaurant, Nailsworth 65 Two Bridges Hotel, Dartmoor
BEST PUB 56 The Swan, Bampton	16 The Longs Arms, Bradford on Avon 17 The Fox, Broughton Gifford
BEST FRONT OF HOUSE TEAM 129 Quies Restaurant at Treglos Hotel, Constantine Bay	15 The Muddy Duck, Bradford on Avon 51 Captain's Club Hotel and Spa, Christchurch
AWARD FOR CREATIVITY AND INNOVATION 5 Wild Garlic Restaurant, Nailsworth	24 The Olive Tree, The Queensberry Hotel, Bath 106 Zacry's at Watergate Bay Hotel
BEST DINE AND STAY EXPERIENCE 72 Soar Mill Cove Hotel and Spa, Salcombe	8 Lucknam Park Hotel and Spa, Colerne 66 Prince Hall Hotel and Restaurant, Dartmoor

THE SOMMELIER: FRIEND OR FOE?

Susy Atkins, BBC One's Saturday Kitchen wine expert thinks the days of trembling over your pronounciation of "viognier" in front of the sommelier are over.

A generation ago, ordering wine in a top restaurant often felt like an ordeal. The sommelier (always a man, and usually buttoned-up, in every sense) was rarely warm or welcoming, sometimes not even remotely helpful. Diners trembling over the pronunciation of "pouilly-fumé" or "viognier" would suffer the sommelier standing over them in silence, poised to take their order, lips pursed in disapproval.

'ALWAYS A MAN, AND USUALLY BUTTONED-UP, IN EVERY SENSE'

Of course I exaggerate a little. But times have changed. Today your sommelier is far more approachable. He - or, almost as likely, she - really does seem to be there to lend a hand.

The best at this delicate job are of course hugely knowledgeable about wine, but that's not all. Nowadays a sommelier must be a whizz at food and wine matching (not easy when the menu constantly changes), and have oodles of tips on the best cocktails, guest beers, latest craft gins, even the merits of mineral versus tap water. And of course they must be adept at serving wine elegantly and knowing when to top up, or when to leave the bottle with the guests.

Which brings me to the often overlooked part of the sommelier's work. It's not enough to have an encyclopedic knowledge of all things "drinks". They must be psychologists as well, sizing up each table of guests and sussing out how best to help them order the right bottle.

They must never talk down to that posh chap who knows (or thinks he knows) his clarets, and they must gently guide a young couple away from ordering the sweet white with the steak.

Elly Owen, head sommelier at Jamie Oliver's Fifteen Cornwall is one of the new breed

They must also make a judgement on the approximate price point a diner finds acceptable - very tricky territory.

As for always handing the wine list to a man - no modern sommelier would dream of such an assumption. It's not difficult to work out, or even ask, who wants to see the list, after all.

The word "sommelier", comes from a French (via Latin) word that meant transporter of goods or, hilariously, animal driver. Clearly it became the word associated with those who supplied the wine to restaurants as I don't think many of us behave like animals when eating out.

We're lucky to have some of the best sommeliers in the world in the South West. We just need to use them a bit more. So make your sommelier work hard. Ask them as many questions as you like: grab some food matching tips; get advice on value for money; find out the best vintage for, say, burgundy on the list.

If you want a smaller glass, a colder sparkler, or a lighter white, let them know. And if a wine tastes wrong or it really isn't to your taste, say so. Then again, if it tastes great, say so as well. Your sommelier could turn out to be a true friend.

'THE WORD "SOMMELIER" MEANT TRANSPORTER OF GOODS ... OR ANIMAL DRIVER'

GASTROPUB SPECIALIST • FLEXIBLE 7-DAY DELIVERY
EXPERTS IN STAFF TRAINING
AWARD WINNING WINES
WINES EXCLUSIVE TO THE ON-TRADE

For a free consultation, including bottles of our 6 best selling wines, email **commercial@majestic.co.uk** and quote 'Trencherman's Guide'.

Wine Specialists
Commercial
majesticcommercial.co.uk

USING THE GUIDE

The Treby Arms **No. 69**

Some restaurants in the guide are accompanied by pictures and more information. These are the Trencherman's establishments that have reached a higher level in the scoring criteria.

All Trencherman's restaurants must meet a very high standard to be included however, so you can be confident that they all offer an exceptional dining experience.

Special places to stay

To find Trencherman's restaurants with rooms, look out for this symbol next to their number.

Trencherman's Awards winners and finalists

Trencherman's members who won a 2016 Trencherman's Award are celebrated throughout the guide with a full page which tells you more about them. You can also identify the finalists by looking for this symbol next to the restaurant's number.

Left: Blow torched scallop, brown shrimp and cockle cocktail, pickled onion gel and burnt apple sauce created by Anton Piotrowski of The Treby Arms (No. 69) for the Trenchermans Awards 2016 dinner.

GLOUCESTERSHIRE

The Slaughters Manor House **No. 1**

1 The Slaughters Manor House
2 The Slaughters Country Inn
3 Lumière
4 The Miners Country Inn
5 Wild Garlic Restaurant

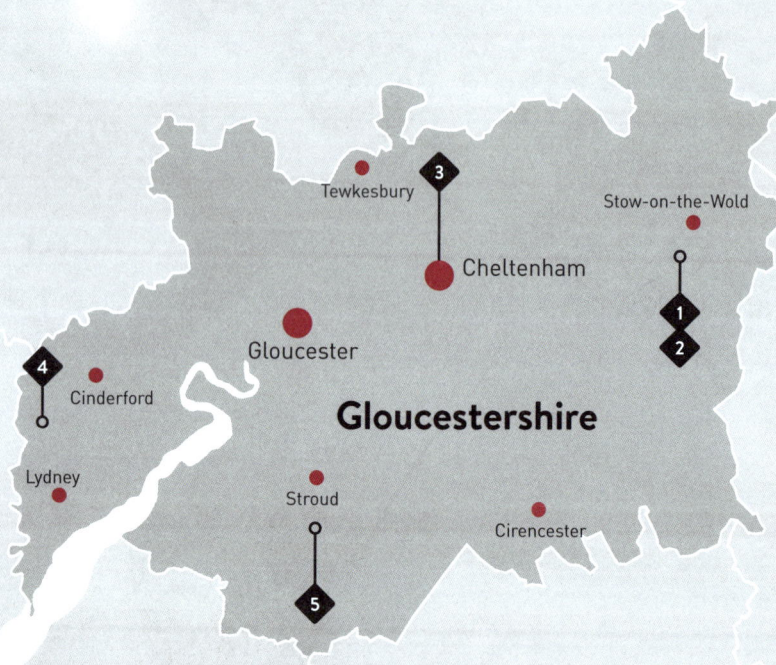

Restaurants listed in the guide correspond to the numbers plotted on the map. Locations are approximate.

New restaurants to the guide are highlighted in red.

1 🔖
The Slaughters Manor House

FINE FOOD WITH COTSWOLD GLAMOUR

A stunning 17th century manor house in arguably one of the country's prettiest villages, The Slaughters Manor House presents a seductive mix of rural glamour, sophisticated interiors and first-class service in the heart of the Cotswolds.

Nineteen luxury bedrooms are complemented by contemporary lounges, manicured gardens and, of course, its three AA rosette restaurant. Seasonal dishes from executive chef Nik Chappell are executed exceedingly well and expertly paired by the resident sommelier with some of the world's finest wines, all enjoyed in the manor's original chapel which now serves as the restaurant.

Chef: **Nik Chappell**
Lunchtime tasting plates from: **£9**
3 course dinner from: **£65**
Seats: **55**
Bedrooms: **19**
Room rate from: **£175**

Lower Slaughter, Gloucestershire, GL54 2HP.
T: 01451 820456

www.slaughtersmanor.co.uk
 The Slaughters Manor House
 @lslaughtersmanor

2 🔖
The Slaughters Country Inn

SOPHISTICATED RURAL CHARM

Country pubs don't come much more picturesque than The Slaughters Country Inn in the village of Lower Slaughter.

Perched on the banks of the River Eye, the golden stone inn oozes rural charm with its roaring log fires and gorgeous sun-drenched grounds.

The finest local produce is the source of head chef Chris Fryer's intriguing mix of sophisticated, seasonal dishes and pub classics, all to be enjoyed within a relaxed and informal setting. And in addition to a good selection of real ales and fine wines, there's a British gin menu to be relished.

Chef: **Chris Fryer**
3 course lunch from: **£22.50**
3 course dinner from: **£29.50**
Seats: **90**
Bedrooms: **31**
Room rate from: **£90**

Lower Slaughter, Gloucestershire, GL54 2HS.
T: 01451 822143

www.theslaughtersinn.co.uk
 The Slaughters Country Inn
 @slaughtersinn

3
Lumière

AWARD WINNING COOKING WITH FLAIR AND FLAVOUR

Jon and Helen Howe's hard work and dedication to fine dining has certainly paid off this year as the husband and wife team secured Lumiere's long awaited third AA rosette.

A contemporary dining space in the centre of Regency Cheltenham, the nearly-hidden restaurant makes for an exceptional lunch stop during a day of chic shopping, as well as a very special intimate dinner date.

Training under an impressive line-up of chefs including Heston Blumenthal and John Campbell, Jon experiments with an exciting mix of complex techniques and classic flavours to create stunning dishes. Try Lumière's nine course tasting menu to really experience the magic.

Chef: **Jon Howe**
3 course lunch from: **£30**
3 course dinner from: **£60**
Seats: **24**

Clarence Parade, Cheltenham, Gloucestershire, GL50 3PA.
T: 01242 222200

www.lumiere.cc
 Lumière Restaurant Cheltenham
 @lumierechelt

4
The Miners Country Inn

RELAXED DINING IN THE FOREST OF DEAN

This is a go-to spot in the Forest of Dean for good food in a relaxed traditional pub setting.

It's welcoming too, being run by husband and wife team Steve and Sam Jenkins, with chef Steve heading up the kitchen.

Proudly sourcing as much produce as possible from within a 10 mile radius of the pub – including rare breed meats, cheeses, vegetables, ales and even butter – the result is daily changing menus to delight.

The inn has multiple awards including maintaining its AA rosette in 2015 and winning a Taste of the West gong.

Chef: **Steven Jenkins**
2 course lunch from: **£9.95**
3 course dinner from: **£14.95**
Seats: **60**
Bedrooms: **4**
Room rate from: **£65**

Chepstow Road, Sling, Coleford, Gloucestershire, GL16 8LH.
T: 01594 836632

www.theminerssling.co.uk
 The Miners Sling
 @theminerssling

5 💲 ◻
Wild Garlic Restaurant

TRENCHERMAN'S AWARDS
AWARD FOR CREATIVITY AND INNOVATION
2016

INNOVATIVE FINE DINING IN THE COTSWOLDS

With a quaint country town setting and a couple of cosy rooms, you'd expect classic Cotswold dining from the kitchen of the Wild Garlic in Nailsworth, but with chef patron Matthew Beardshall at the helm, that certainly isn't so.

Opening the restaurant with rooms in 2007 with wife Hannah, Matthew crafts ingenious menus using seasonal ingredients and inventive cookery techniques. The tasting menu is a must on any visit to this intimate dining space, and general manager Henry Bannister's hand-picked wine flight is a delight to sample along the way. There are also three charming bedrooms upstairs if Henry's selection of artisan aperitifs prove too tempting.

Chef: **Matthew Beardshall**
3 course set lunch: **£25**
3 course dinner from: **£25**
Seats: **29**
Bedrooms: **3**
Room rate from: **£95**

GLOUCESTERSHIRE

3 Cossack Square, Nailsworth, Gloucestershire, GL6 0DB.
T: 01453 832615

www.wild-garlic.co.uk

 Wild Garlic Restaurant & Rooms    @thewildgarlic   @wildgarlicnailsworth

WILTSHIRE

Howard's House **No. 10**

6 The Bell at Ramsbury
7 The Pear Tree at Purton
8 Lucknam Park Hotel and Spa
9 The Methuen Arms
10 Howard's House
11 Three Tuns Freehouse
12 The Old House at Home
13 The Castle Inn Hotel
14 The Northey Arms
15 The Muddy Duck
16 The Longs Arms
17 The Fox
18 Three Daggers

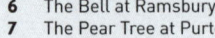

Restaurants listed in the guide correspond to the numbers plotted on the map. Locations are approximate.

New restaurants to the guide are highlighted in red.

6

The Bell at Ramsbury

LIVE THE WILTSHIRE GOOD LIFE

The Bell sits on the village square at Ramsbury and has been carefully renovated to combine the 300-year-old former coaching inn's original features with contemporary elements and its nine lovely bedrooms.

Then there's the Ramsbury estate, which produces and supplies game, real ale and the cold pressed rapeseed oil which chef Jonus Lodge and the team use in the bar and kitchen. It's self sufficiency all the way as Jonus also makes full use of the walled kitchen garden in menus that range from classic pub food to rather special fine dining.

Chef: **Jonus Lodge**
3 course lunch from: **£24**
3 course dinner from: **£24**
Seats: **42**
Bedrooms: **9**
Room rate from: **£110**

The Square, Ramsbury, Wiltshire, SN8 2PE.
T: 01672 520230

www.thebellramsbury.com

- The Bell at Ramsbury
- @thebellramsbury
- @bell_ramsbury

7

The Pear Tree at Purton

WINE AND WILDFLOWERS

A former vicarage, this small, family run country house hotel is gloriously set in seven and a half acres of gardens, which include its own vineyard.

Needless to say there's ample opportunity to sample the wines, and who wouldn't want to sip a glass of its Cuvee Anne sparkling wine while sitting in the elegant Conservatory Restaurant, in the formal garden that surrounds the house.

Explore the wildflower meadows and take a peek at the beehives before sampling dishes from chef Adam Conduit's modern English menu.

Chef: **Adam Conduit**
3 course lunch from: **£22**
3 course dinner from: **£33**
Seats: **50**
Bedrooms: **17**
Room rate from: **£109**

Church End, Purton, near Swindon, Wiltshire, SN5 4ED.
T: 01793 772100

www.peartreepurton.co.uk

- The Pear Tree at Purton
- @purtonpeartree

8 Luckman Park Hotel and Spa

SHEER GLAMOUR IN THE COUNTRYSIDE

Undoubtedly one of the South West's most glamorous dining destinations, this fabulous hotel and spa is alluring inside and out. Fine furnishings, silk wallpapers, objet d'art and exquisite flowers inside the Palladian mansion are echoed in 500 acres of stunning parkland and gardens.

It's thoroughly fitting then that head chef Hywel Jones creates such a sumptuous dining experience at the Michelin starred Park Restaurant. Start with cocktails and canapés in the drawing room, thrill to Jones' five rosette menus, crafted using organic ingredients from the kitchen garden and luxuriate in fine wines suggested by the sommelier. All of this, plus impressive spa facilities and a contemporary brasserie make Lucknam a must-visit.

Chef: **Hywel Jones**
3 course Sunday lunch from: **£39**
3 course dinner from: **£80**
Seats: **64**
Bedrooms: **42**
Room rate from: **£290**

Colerne, Chippenham, Wiltshire, SN14 8AZ.
T: 01225 742777

www.lucknampark.co.uk
- Lucknam Park Hotel & Spa
- @lucknampark
- @lucknam_park

9 The Methuen Arms

A DASH OF ITALIAN AT A CHARMING GEORGIAN INN

It's a delight to visit this beautifully restored Georgian inn. Exposed stone walls, wooden floors and log fires, along with decorative touches, indicate the serious amount of care that's gone in to the building – an ethos that's reflected in the quality of food.

Simple, classic dishes using seasonal ingredients with a refreshing dash of Italian influence are the order of the day – and at excellent prices too.

Choose between different eating areas including a snug, garden view restaurant or pretty courtyard for alfresco dining. Next to the stately home of Corsham Court, it's also a great base from which to explore the Wiltshire and Somerset countryside.

Chef: **Piero Boi**
3 course lunch from: **£21.50**
3 course dinner from: **£35**
Seats: **80**
Bedrooms: **14**
Room rate from: **£130**

2 High Street, Corsham, Wiltshire, SN13 0HB.
T: 01249 717060

www.themethuenarms.com
- The Methuen Arms
- @methuenarms
- @themethuenarms

10
Howard's House

GOURMET ESCAPE IN BLISSFUL WILTSHIRE COUNTRYSIDE

Tucked away in the Nadder Valley's rolling hills, Howard's House Hotel is the stuff of rural dreams.

The Grade II-listed country house in the pretty village of Teffont Evias has nine unique and cosy bedrooms, as well as an impressive restaurant headed up by chef Nick Wentworth.

Nick's close links with local producers pays off in an exquisite menu of seasonal British dishes, and there's a healthy wine cellar to complement his work. Serious gastronomists should make a bee-line for the Gourmet Getaway which includes a bespoke seven course menu tailored to individual tastes.

Chef: **Nick Wentworth**
3 course lunch from: **£20**
3 course dinner from: **£32.50**
Seats: **22**
Bedrooms: **9**
Room rate from: **£190 (double)**

Teffont Evias, Salisbury, Wiltshire, SP3 5RJ.
T: 01722 716392

www.howardshousehotel.co.uk

Howard's House Hotel
@howards_house

TRENCHERMAN'S COLLECTIONS

Take five country dining pubs

56 The Swan, Bampton
This year's Trencherman's Awards Best Pub is the perfect stop after a stomp on Exmoor.

17 The Fox, Broughton Gifford
Homegrown goodies and easy going service are just two reasons to visit this alluring Wiltshire pub.

26 The Wheatsheaf Combe Hay
Rustic interiors with a crackling fire in winter, and tiered gardens, beehives and veg patch in summer. What's not to love?

27 The Pony & Trap, Chew Magna
Josh Eggleton's Michelin-starred dining pub celebrates 10 years of creative cooking.

36 The Queens Arms, Corton Denham
Dig in to top notch food, homemade scotch eggs and a hangover-worthy array of drinks just off the A303.

WILTSHIRE

11
Three Tuns Freehouse

Since re-opening in 2012, chef patron James Wilsey and his wife Ashley have grown quite a foodie following at this traditional village pub on the Wiltshire/Berkshire border. With a daily changing à la carte menu, diners can enjoy the freshest seasonal ingredients gracing the plates, with everything from bread to horseradish sauce handmade by its band of chefs. There's a relaxed bar menu all day, plus perfectly conditioned local ales and a wine list worth taking time over.

Chef: **James Wilsey**. 3 course lunch from: **£25**. 3 course dinner from: **£25**. Seats: **50**.

1 High Street, Great Bedwyn, Marlborough, Wiltshire, SN8 3NU.
T: 01672 870280

www.threetunsbedwyn.co.uk

- The Three Tuns Freehouse, Great Bedwyn
- @threetunsbedwyn
- @three_tuns_bedwyn

12
The Old House at Home

A historic ivy-clad country inn complete with original oak beams and roaring open fires, The Old House at Home is a quintessential Wiltshire pub. Located just a couple of miles from Castle Combe, the family-run restaurant in the village of Burton offers visitors cracking classics like Saxon Splendour sausages with mustard mash, alongside more refined options such as grilled sea bass and tiger prawn linguine. And six cosy bedrooms above the inn provide an opportunity to sample sommelier Matt Warburton's impressive list.

Chef: **Chris Alderson**. 3 course lunch from: **£16**. 3 course dinner from: **£26**. Seats: **70**. Bedrooms: **6**. Room rate from: **£85**

Burton, near Castle Combe, Wiltshire, SN14 7LT.
T: 01454 218227

www.ohhpubs.co.uk

- The OHH Pub Company
- @ohhpubs

13
The Castle Inn Hotel

This beautiful Cotswold stone inn, whose origins can be traced back to the 12th century, is in one of England's prettiest villages. Its owners have made the most of its original features, carefully restoring them as part of a major renovation of the building. Just as much attention is paid to the food which is created by new head chef George Sirbu who continues to build on the inn's culinary credentials. There's a range of eating options from traditional bar meals to à la carte dining.

Chef: **George Sirbu**. 3 course lunch from: **£25.95**. 3 course dinner from: **£27.50**. Seats: **46**. Bedrooms: **11**. Room rate from: **£135**

Castle Combe, near Chippenham, Wiltshire, SN14 7HN.

T: 01249 783030

www.castle-inn.info

- The Castle Inn Hotel - Castle Combe
- @castleinnccombe
- @castleinncastlecombe

14
The Northey Arms

This appealing Bath stone pub in the historic village of Box has been winning even more fans since it underwent renovation recently. Formerly the Box Station Hotel, it owes its architecture to Brunel and its impressive food to chef Chris Alderson. The menu is classic and seasonal, with fish from Cornwall and locally sourced beef. Stylish bedrooms, complete with artworks and slate stone bathrooms, along with the pub's close location to Bath, makes it a great find for a foodie stay near the city.

Chef: **Chris Alderson**. 3 course lunch from: **£16**. 3 course dinner from: **£26**. Seats: **75**. Bedrooms: **10**. Room rate from: **£85**

Bath Road, Box, Wiltshire, SN13 8AE.

T: 01225 742333

www.ohhpubs.co.uk

- The OHH Pub Company
- @ohhpubs

INSIDER'S TIP

'I love tasting menus and tapas – lots of small bites of different flavours. I enjoy eating at The Bath Priory (No. 21) as its tasting menus are excellent.'

Nick Wentworth, head chef, Howard's House **No. 10**

TotalProduce

Suppliers of Quality Fresh Produce to the Catering Trade

www.totalproducelocal.co.uk

Local at Heart, Global by Nature

15
The Muddy Duck

Heralded as Wiltshire's most haunted pub, thankfully there's nothing scary about the gastronomic offerings at The Muddy Duck. The 17th century country inn has been given a contemporary makeover, with a relaxed bar area with cosy snugs for snacks, sandwiches and casual drinks, as well as its more formal restaurant in which to sample head chef Josh Roberts' cooking. Expect flavours from around the world on a concise dining menu, plus a well-thought-out wine list to match. Then stay above the pub - if you dare.

Chef: **Josh Roberts**. 3 course lunch from: **£18**. 3 course dinner from: **£22**. Seats: **50**. Bedrooms: **5**. Room rate from: **£125**

42 Monkton Farleigh, Bradford on Avon, Wiltshire, BA15 2QH.

T: 01225 858705

www.themuddyduckbath.co.uk

- The Muddy Duck, Monkton Farleigh
- @muddyduckbath
- @muddyduckbath

17
The Fox

The accolades of Trencherman's Best Pub 2015 and runner up in 2016, say much about this foodie dining pub in the Wiltshire countryside.

Using its own smallholding to grow some of the food for the sophisticated but pleasingly rustic menus, expect homemade charcuterie and free range produce. A dynamic young team delivers excellence with simplicity and makes this a must-visit. You can even stay in its luxurious apartment across the road.

Chef: **Peter Arrowsmith**. 3 course lunch from: **£18**. 3 course dinner from: **£25**. Seats: **40**. Bedrooms: **1**. Room rate from: **£125**

The Street, Broughton Gifford, Melksham, Wiltshire, SN12 8PN.

T: 01225 782949

www.thefox-broughtongifford.co.uk

- @thefoxbroughton
- @thefoxbroughton

16
The Longs Arms

This striking, old stone pub in the village of South Wraxall (between Bath and Bradford on Avon), comes with a great choice of cask ales, super seasonal food, dyed-in-the-wool rustic charm and a warm welcome from the landlord - who's also an award winning chef. Its own smokehouse creates extra excitement on the menu, and everything here is made in-house, from bread to chocs. It's hard to know whether to cosy up inside or eat alfresco in the pretty walled garden; so let the weather decide and save the decision making for a menu that merits the "local" label through and through.

Chef: **Robert Allcock**. 3 course lunch from: **£28**. 3 course dinner from: **£28**. Seats: **36**

South Wraxall, Bradford on Avon, Wiltshire, BA15 2SB.

T: 01225 864450

www.thelongsarms.com

- The Longs Arms
- @thelongsarms

18
Three Daggers

With fruit and veg from its own farm stocking the kitchen and real ale from the house brewery in the bar, this popular village inn takes pride in keeping things local.

Taking classic pub dining up a notch, head chef Kevin Chandler creates a winning line-up of seasonal dishes such as chicken livers, black pudding and bacon on toast, and monkfish tails, pink fir apples and wild mushrooms. There's always something going on – from live music to tasting evenings, plus there are three cosy bedrooms.

Chef: **Kevin Chandler**. 3 course lunch from: **£23**. 3 course dinner from: **£45**. Seats: **45**. Bedrooms: **3**. Room rate from: **£105**

47 Westbury Road, Edington, Westbury, Wiltshire, BA13 4PG.

T: 01380 830940

www.threedaggers.co.uk

- The Three Daggers
- @3daggers
- @3daggers

BATH & BRISTOL

The Pony & Trap **No. 27**

19 Harvey Nichols Second Floor Restaurant
20 Casamia
21 The Bath Priory
22 The Marlborough Tavern
23 The Chequers
24 The Olive Tree
25 Menu Gordon Jones
26 The Wheatsheaf Combe Hay
27 The Pony & Trap
28 The Kensington Arms
29 The Mint Room - Bristol
30 The Mint Room - Bath
31 Combe Grove
32 The Bear and Swan

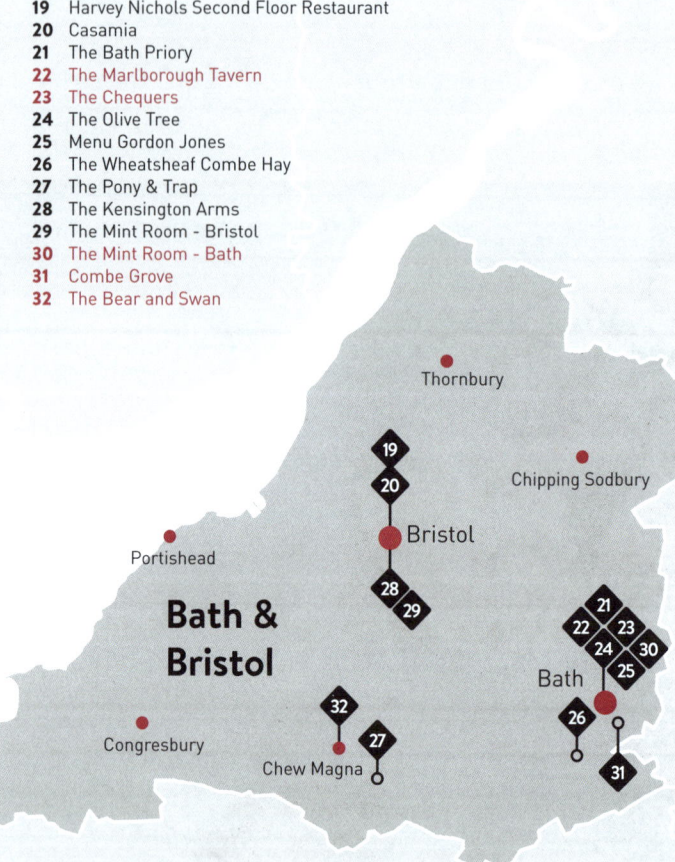

Restaurants listed in the guide correspond to the numbers plotted on the map. Locations are approximate.

New restaurants to the guide are highlighted in red.

19
Harvey Nichols Second Floor Restaurant

MCCRIMMON'S MIDAS TOUCH

You can't talk about Harvey Nichols' Bristol restaurant without mentioning the gold. Fabulous gold leather banquettes and shimmering metallic fabrics used in a restrained, contemporary way make this large, buzzy restaurant feel as special as the garments displayed on the floor below.

The set menu is incredible value at £17 for two and £20 for three courses, but head chef Louise McCrimmon's à la carte menus are the real haute couture, showcasing modern British cooking with classical influences from breakfast to dinner.

Chef: **Louise McCrimmon**
3 course lunch from: **£20**
3 course dinner from: **£20**
Seats: **60**

20
Casamia

EXCEPTIONAL DINING ON BRISTOL'S HARBOURSIDE

Moving to a fresh new venue in the belly of the city's former General Hospital at the start of 2016 marks a new chapter for Casamia and the Sanchez Brothers brand.

Highly innovative, Michelin-starred cooking is served as a ten course tasting menu - six at lunch - in slick, pared-back surroundings. Every dish from head chef Peter Sanchez-Iglesias and his team of talented chefs in the theatre kitchen is crafted with precision, the influence of the seasons and local produce embodied in the bold flavours of each course.

Indulge in the matched wine flight too – cooking this good deserves a strong supporting cast to highlight the star of the show.

Photo: John Blackwell

Chef: **Peter Sanchez-Iglesias**
6 course lunch from: **£38**
10 course dinner from: **£68**
Seats: **40**

---

27 Philadelphia Street, Bristol, BS1 3BZ.
T: 01179 168898

www.harveynichols.com

- Harvey Nichols
- @harveynichols
- @harveynichols

The General, Lower Guinea Street, Bristol, BS1 6SY.
T: 01179 592884

www.casamiarestaurant.co.uk

- Casamia
- @casamia_
- @casamiabristol

21 💲
The Bath Priory

STYLE AND GLAMOUR IN A GEORGIAN MANSION

A haven of quintessential English style and glamour, and just a short stroll through the park from Bath's bustling city centre, this is a must-visit for gourmet travellers.

The late Georgian stone mansion sits in four acres of award winning gardens and is home to Michelin-starred executive chef Sam Moody. Sam and his brigade take guests on a memorable culinary journey with modern British menus crafted from fresh local produce.

For the full experience, start dinner with an aperitif on the flower-filled terrace, enjoy views of the garden as you dine in the restaurant and stay the night in a luxurious bedroom.

Chef: **Sam Moody**
3 course lunch from: **£30**
3 course dinner from: **£80**
Seats: **56**
Bedrooms: **33**
Room rate from: **£195**

Weston Road, Bath, Somerset, BA1 2XT.
T: 01225 331922

www.thebathpriory.co.uk
- The Bath Priory Hotel, Restaurant & Spa
- @thebathpriory

22
The Marlborough Tavern

SMART, CLASSIC BRITISH COOKING DOWN THE PUB

This stylish dining pub with its very modern approach to food is in the centre of Georgian Bath, just a stone's throw from the world famous Royal Crescent.

With its muted tones and simple dark wood furniture, it's a pleasure to sit and sample from the range of real ales, but with two AA rosette cooking, the menu really has to be explored. Solidly British in theme, this is heartwarming, freshly made food using well sourced, quality ingredients, with a good dose of creative flair from chef Daniel Edwards.

Don't miss a chance to sit in the outdoor courtyard and make sure to book for the very popular Sunday roasts which have people fighting for a table.

Chef: **Daniel Edwards**
3 course lunch from: **£16**
3 course dinner from: **£26**
Seats: **75**

35 Marlborough Buildings, Bath, Somerset, BA1 2LY.
T: 01225 423731

www.marlborough-tavern.com
- The Marlborough Tavern, Bath
- @marlboroughtav
- @marlboroughtavern

23
The Chequers

CRACKING GASTROPUB IN THE CITY

Established in 1776, The Chequers is a beautifully appointed gastropub, serving award winning, inventive British food in a friendly pub atmosphere.

The menu is progressive, but with a nod to the pub's heritage in the shape of perfectly executed classic British dishes. Head chef Tony Casey's excellent palate and focus on the finest produce comes through in the way each dish tastes and is presented.

The service is knowledgeable but friendly, and there's an extensive, interesting and diverse wine list to accompany.

Chef: **Tony Casey**
3 course lunch from: **£26 (Saturday and Sunday only)**
3 course dinner from: **£30**
Seats: **70**

50 Rivers Street, Bath, Somerset, BA1 2QA.
T: 01225 360017

www.chequersbath.com

- The Chequers, Bath
- @chequersbath
- @chequersbath

24
The Olive Tree

EXQUISITE COOKING AT AN ALMOST HIDDEN LOCATION

Located in a quiet street in the heart of Georgian Bath, The Olive Tree is one of the city's longest established and most highly decorated independent restaurants.

With an air of the gentleman's club about it, and occupying several basement rooms in the smart Queensberry Hotel, it's like stumbling across a secret delight, no matter how often you visit. But there's nothing traditional or stuffy about either the decor - it was beautifully refurbished last year - or the cooking.

Head chef Chris Cleghorn, who trained with three world-renowned Michelin chefs, brings an extraordinary intensity of seasonal flavours to every dish he meticulously crafts - and he's always discovering something new. This is informal fine dining at its best.

Chef: **Chris Cleghorn**
3 course lunch from: **£30**
3 course dinner from: **£50**
Seats: **50**
Bedrooms: **29**
Room rate from: **£125**

The Queensberry Hotel, 4-7 Russel Street, Bath, Somerset, BA1 2QF.
T: 01225 447928

www.olivetreebath.co.uk

- Olive Tree, Bath
- @olivetreebath
- @chriscleghornolivetree

25

Menu Gordon Jones
CREATIVE COOKERY IN THE HEART OF BATH

Menu Gordon Jones probably isn't a restaurant that you'll be visiting anytime soon – unless you already have a booking - as the 20 cover restaurant has a lengthy waiting list.

Don't let this put you off though, as the food from Michelin-trained chef Gordon Jones is well worth the wait. Inclusion in the *Sunday Times*' Top 100 Restaurants list, and a Trencherman's Award for Creativity and Innovation certainly warrants its popularity. Dining at this Bath restaurant is an event to savour, with each course of chef's ingenious secret menus revealed for the first time as the dishes reach the table - every one a piece of art.

Chef: **Gordon Jones**
5 course tasting: **£45**
6 course tasting: **£55**
Seats: **22**

2 Wellsway, Bath, Somerset, BA2 3AQ.
T: 01225 480871

www.menugordonjones.co.uk

Menu Gordon Jones
@menugordonjones

26

The Wheatsheaf Combe Hay
TOP QUALITY COUNTRY DINING

A little slice of the country just 10 minutes from Bath, The Wheatsheaf Combe Hay encompasses all the best bits of the traditional pub – great food, fine wine and a friendly welcome.

The menu from head chef Eddie Rains changes with the seasons, so guests can look forward to British classics like beef shin with peppercorn sauce served by the fire in winter, and lighter dishes such as the Brixham crab salad on the sun-drenched terrace come summer. Keep an eye on its website for gourmet events and tasting evenings.

Chef: **Eddy Rains**
3 course lunch from: **£21**
3 course dinner from: **£23**
Seats: **50**
Bedrooms: **3**
Room rate from: **£120**

Combe Hay, Bath, Somerset, BA2 7EG.
T: 01225 833504

www.wheatsheafcombehay.com

27
The Pony & Trap

A DECADE OF CREATIVE COOKING

This year, siblings Josh and Holly Eggleton celebrate ten years at their Chew Magna dining pub, and it's the culmination of huge success for the hard working pair.

Heading up the kitchen, Josh's creative cooking is rooted in British traditions and has helped the pub earn a Michelin star every year since 2011 and second place in the *Publican Morning Advertiser's* Top 50 Gastropubs in 2015, while Holly won its Front of House of the Year award in 2014.

The winning team goes the extra mile to create intriguing gourmet experiences and regular special events such as the Spice of Britain tasting night, themed around the great British curry. Consequently, it's very popular, but if you can't get in, console yourself at its nearby fish and chip shop, Salt and Malt.

Chef: **Josh Eggleton**
3 course lunch from: **£35**
3 course dinner from: **£49**
Seats: **65**

Knowle Hill, Newton, Chew Magna, Bristol, BS40 8TQ.
T: 01275 332627

www.theponyandtrap.co.uk

- The Pony & Trap
- @theponyandtrap
- @theponyandtrap

TRENCHERMAN'S COLLECTIONS

Take five unusual dining experiences

47 Crab House Cafe
Slurp fresh oysters, harvested from the cafe's own oyster beds just metres from your table, within minutes of them leaving the water.

25 Menu Gordon Jones
The wildly innovative chef keeps an air of mystery around his tasting menus, so you won't know what you'll be eating until it arrives.

20 Casamia
The creative ten course tasting menu is the order of the day at Casamia's new home at Bristol's former eye hospital.

71 Glazebrook House Hotel
There's a surprise around every corner at this theatrical boutique hotel. Book ahead to dine in Anton Piotrowski's chef's kitchen and follow with a tutored whisky tasting.

29 & 30 The Mint Room
Fine dining execution and presentation meets authentic Indian cuisine at the contemporary Mint Rooms in Bath and Bristol.

BATH & BRISTOL

28
The Kensington Arms

The owners of this Bristol pub and restaurant are firm believers in the term "public house", and want visitors to arrive, eat, drink and relax like they're in a home from home. And as a result, the Kenny (as the customers call it), is every bit a local fave.

This might be a pub but chef Charlie runs a traditional kitchen where the bread's baked daily and butchery done on site. Expect simple, honest food in a family and dog-friendly local.

Chef: **Charlie Hearn**. 3 course lunch from: **£20**. 3 course dinner from: **£22**. Seats: **38**

35-37 Stanley Road, Redland, Bristol, BS6 6NP.
T: 01179 446444

www.thekensingtonarms.co.uk

- Kensington Arms
- @kensingtonarms

29
The Mint Room

With its contemporary interpretation of traditional Indian cuisine, The Mint Room offers Bristol's gourmets a refreshing take on fine dining. From a prime position on Clifton Road, picture-perfect plates coming from the kitchen of this sleek restaurant make good company for its gastronomic neighbours. Wines are carefully matched to each of chef Saravanan's intriguing dishes by the in-house sommelier, and there's a champagne lounge for pre-dinner drinks when the occasion calls.

Chef: **Saravanan Nimbarajan**. 3 course lunch from: **£15**. 3 course dinner from: **£25**. Seats: **80**

12-16 Clifton Road, Bristol, BS8 1AF.
T: 01173 291300

www.themintroom.co.uk

- The Mint Room
- @themintroom
- @themintroom

30
The Mint Room

This is the in-place in Bath for fabulous fine dining, Indian-style. The award winning restaurant focuses on traditional and regional cuisine, prepared and served with a modern twist. Drawing on a wealth of culinary experience - its chefs hail from some of the top restaurants in London and India - you'll find signature dishes with varying degrees and levels of spiciness. The contemporary setting and excellent wine list also adds to the charming experience.

Chef: **Soyful Alom**. 3 course lunch from: **£15**. 3 course dinner from: **£25**. Seats: **80**

Longmead, Gospel Hall, Lower Bristol Road, Bath, BA2 3EB.

T: 01225 446656

www.themintroom.co.uk

 The Mint Room
 @themintroom
 @themintroom

31
Combe Grove

Award winning young chef Leigh Evans – previously of acclaimed Bath dining pub The Chequers – leads the kitchen team at this beautiful country house set in 70 acres, minutes from the heart of the city. Leigh's culinary style favours the local, flavoursome and healthy and yet he's not afraid to be bold in his menus. Expect contemporary, feel-good food that looks as good as it tastes. With rooms, spa, leisure club, indoor and outdoor pools and tennis facilities, its also a great place to stay. Scullery is open for all day casual dining, too.

Chef: **Leigh Evans**. 2 course Sunday lunch from: **£21**. 3 course dinner from: **£37.50**. Seats: **36**. Bedrooms: **40**. Room rate from: **£120**

Brassknocker Hill, Bath, Avon, BA2 7HS.
T: 01225 834644

www.combegrove.com

 Combe Grove
 @combegrove

32
The Bear and Swan

In the rolling Mendip Hills, The Bear and Swan is close enough to bustling Bristol for an evening escape, yet secluded enough to warrant a weekend break. Housed in a traditional 18th century inn, the pub with six boutique rooms offers a classic country dining experience, with roaring fires and cosy candlelit corners. Chef Chris Alderson caters to the pub's wide range of visitors, from hearty sandwiches for weary walkers to superb soufflés and fresh tagliatelle for date night diners.

Chef: **Chris Alderson**. 3 course lunch from: **£16**. 3 course dinner from: **£26**. Seats: **70**. Bedrooms: **6**. Room rate from: **£85**

13 South Parade, Chew Magna, Bristol, BS40 8PR.

T: 01275 331100

www.ohhpubs.co.uk

 The OHH Pub Company
 @ohhpubs

BATH & BRISTOL

SOMERSET

Little Barwick House **No. 37**

33 Goodfellows Restaurant
34 The Pilgrims Restaurant
35 The Cedar Restaurant
36 The Queens Arms
37 Little Barwick House
38 Augustus
39 The Restaurant @ Centurion
40 Psalter's Restaurant at The Luttrell Arms
41 The Rising Sun Inn
42 The Globe

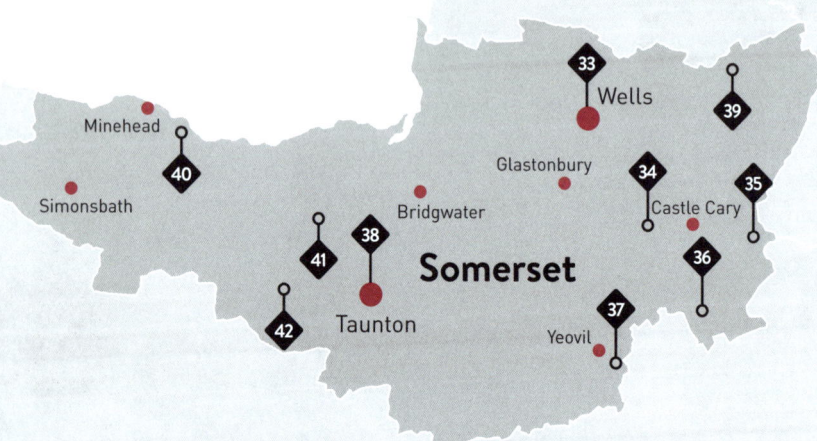

Restaurants listed in the guide correspond to the numbers plotted on the map. Locations are approximate.

New restaurants to the guide are highlighted in red.

33
Goodfellows Restaurant

THEATRE OF DELIGHT IN WELLS

Adam Fellows is a creative, talented chef who has been feeding the good food lovers of Wells exceedingly well for many years. With inspiration from the Med and using spankingly fresh fish caught off the coast of Devon and Cornwall, you can expect beautiful food and smart service, care of Adam's wife Martine and compatriot Renuad who run the front of house.

Diners can enjoy a dash of theatre with their gourmet delights, courtesy of the open kitchen that's captured on camera and displayed on flat screens around the joint. Visit in the daytime for the more relaxed cafe menu.

Chef: **Adam Fellows**
3 course lunch from: **£23.50**
3 course dinner from: **£30**
Seats: **35**

34 ⓢ
The Pilgrims Restaurant

TRUE DESTINATION DINING

In the heart of the Somerset countryside, Jools Mitchison holds good to his promise that everything he serves has its origins 'just out there' i.e. a few metres from his front door.

He takes as much delight in hunting down some of the county's best, and typically modest, growers and producers, as he does in creating his own unique dishes.

This passion for Somerset means the accomplished chef has never lost touch with what makes food good: 'It's not about me,' he insists, 'it's about the stunning ingredients'.

Chef: **Jools Mitchison**
3 course lunch from: **£26**
3 course dinner from: **£28**
Seats: **25**
Bedrooms: **5**
Room rate from: **£80**

5 Sadler Street, Wells, Somerset, BA5 2RR.
T: 01749 673866

www.goodfellowswells.co.uk

 Goodfellows Restaurant, Wells
 @goodfellowseat

Pilgrims Way, Lovington, Castle Cary, Somerset, BA7 7PT.
T: 01963 240597

www.thepilgrimsatlovington.co.uk

 The Pilgrims at Lovington
 @pilgrimskitchen
 @pilgrimskitchen

forest produce

SPECIALIST INGREDIENTS FOR CHEFS

DELIVERING 5 DAYS

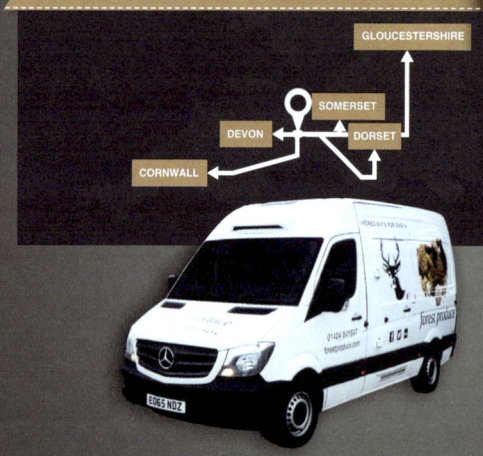

01404 841847

forestproduce.com

35

The Cedar Restaurant

MODERN COOKING AMID COUNTRY HOUSE GLAMOUR

Just off the A303, The Cedar Restaurant at Holbrook House Hotel is a wonderful escape from the bustle of modern life. A cornucopia of polished dark wood, crackling fires, wall mounted stags' heads and gleaming silver cloches makes this country house hotel seductive in a P G Wodehouse kind of way.

Start the evening with a glass of something good from the extensive wine list with canapés in front of the fire, before moving into a dining room of delicious faded grandeur for very accomplished modern British cooking from new head chef Paul Hudson. Desserts are particularly good, so make sure you save room.

Chef: **Paul Hudson**
3 course lunch from: **£20**
3 course dinner from: **£45**
Seats: **80**
Bedrooms: **21**
Room rate from: **£95**

Holbrook House, Wincanton, Somerset, BA9 8BS.
T: 01963 824466

www.holbrookhouse.co.uk

- Holbrook House
- @holbrookhouse
- @holbrookhouse

36

The Queens Arms

HISTORIC INN WITH PLENTY OF DINING SURPRISES

This 18th century dining inn just off the A303 is a great gourmet pit stop as well as a very popular dine and stay destination in its own right.

The delight is in the detail here, and it shows in every element, from the homemade sloe gin and pork pies piled up on the bar, to the sophisticated restaurant fare in which everything – including ice cream, bread and preserves - is made by head chef Dan Richards and his team of five chefs.

As with the food, the rooms are high quality and attractive, with more lovely touches such as quality toiletries, a huge array of films to watch and little treats.

Chef: **Dan Richards**
3 course lunch from: **£25**
3 course dinner from: **£35**
Seats: **78**
Bedrooms: **8**
Room rate from: **£85**

Corton Denham, Sherborne, Somerset, DT9 4LR.
T: 01963 220317

www.thequeensarms.com

- The Queens Arms Pub - Corton Denham, Somerset
- @queensarmspub
- @queensarmspub

The Luttrell Arms **No. 40**

37
Little Barwick House

A VERY SPECIAL STAY WITH THE FORD FAMILY

Tucked into the curve of an old Somerset lane, this elegant house set in a tree and flower filled garden has been in the hands of Tim and Emma Ford for almost two decades.

Their joint culinary and hospitality credentials are evident throughout this immaculately kept, but oh so cosy and comfortable restaurant with rooms - so it's no surprise that it's held three AA rosettes since the day it opened.

Tim, with the help of son Olly, effortlessly creates classic dishes with a modern twist, and make sure you sample something from wine expert Emma's extensive list, which includes many great wines by the glass, including Krug champagne.

Chef: **Tim Ford**
3 course lunch from: **£29.95**
3 course dinner from: **£49.95**
Seats: **44**
Bedrooms: **7**
Room rate from: **£120**

Rexes Hollow Lane, Barwick, near Yeovil, Somerset, BA22 9TD.
T: 01935 423902

www.littlebarwickhouse.co.uk

- Little Barwick House
- @littlebarwick
- @littlebarwickhouse

38
Augustus

INTERNATIONAL COOKING AT TAUNTON'S HIDDEN GEM

You'll discover in-the-know locals and Taunton's sharp-eared tourists at this laid-back little bistro that's hidden away in a courtyard near the town centre.

Classically trained head chef Richard Guest tempts loyal followers with an intriguing range of British, French and Asian fusion dishes, while front of house, Cedric Chirossel woos with charming service and fine wines.

A pleasing clash of cultures on the ever-changing menu ensures a unique experience at every visit – from traditional Somerset faggots to venison parmentier.

Chef: **Richard Guest**
3 course lunch from: **£28**
3 course dinner from: **£28**
Seats: **38**

3 The Courtyard, St James Street, Taunton, Somerset, TA1 1JR.
T: 01823 324354

www.augustustaunton.com

- Augustus Restaurant
- @augustustaunton

SOMERSET

39
The Restaurant @ Centurion

Overlooking extensive hotel gardens, the restaurant at the Centurion hotel is a perfect place for spacious, relaxed dining. The hotel itself offers plenty of superb amenities - pool, sauna, steam room, jacuzzi, gym and even a nine hole golf course - and it's great to find an equal amount of attention paid to its food offering. Expect well cooked seasonal offerings from chef Sean Horwood and team.

Chef: **Sean Horwood**. 3 course lunch from: **£17**. 3 course dinner from: **£27**. Seats: **60**. Bedrooms: **45**. Room rate from: **£87.50**

Charlton Lane, Midsomer Norton, Radstock, Somerset, BA3 4BD.
T: 01761 412214

www.centurionhotel.co.uk

- The Restaurant at Centurion
- @restatcent
- @restatcent

40
Psalter's Restaurant at The Luttrell Arms

A must-visit on Exmoor, The Luttrell Arms is a historic, quirky venue that combines a traditional bar, stylish lounge, fabulous beer garden (with views of Dunster Castle) and comfy rooms. Great for weary travellers, it's the fine dining restaurant which is the draw for visiting foodies, with seasonal dishes and specialities such as local game expertly crafted by head chef, Barry Tucker.

Chef: **Barry Tucker**. 3 course lunch from: **£16.95**. 3 course dinner from: **£29**. Seats: **45**. Bedrooms: **28**. Room rate from: **£100**

The Luttrell Arms Hotel, 32-36 High Street, Dunster, Somerset, TA24 6SG.
T: 01643 821555

www.luttrellarms.co.uk

- The Luttrell Arms Hotel
- @psaltersdining

41
The Rising Sun Inn

This charming dining pub in the Quantocks is cosy and unpretentious with a lovely old oak bar, flagstone flooring, beamed ceiling and antique furniture. New owner Linda Palk, manager/chef Amanda Palk and head chef Anthony Michael Hohmann continue the inn's tradition of classic, high quality pub food, also serving fresh sustainable fish dishes such as wild sea bass with artichoke puree. Choose from a number of rooms in which to dine and check out the well priced wine list. It's next to two walking trails, and dogs are welcome too.

Chef: **Anthony Michael Hohmann**. 3 course lunch from: **£25**. 3 course dinner from: **£35**. Seats: **65**. Bedrooms: **2**. Room rate from: **£95**

West Bagborough, Taunton, Somerset, TA4 3EF.
T: 01823 432575

www.risingsuninn.info

Somerset Rising Sun Inn

42
The Globe

Now celebrating 10 years at The Globe, Mark and Adele Tarry have successfully turned this 18th century coaching inn at the heart of the Somerset village of Milverton into a popular and well priced place to dine. Step inside the elegant, Grade II-listed building and you'll find a contemporary and stylish interior. From bar snacks and hearty classics to more refined dining, it's all about the quality, home cooked food. Look out for special dining nights.

Chef: **Mark Tarry**. 3 course lunch from: **£23**. 3 course dinner from: **£23**. Seats: **40**. Bedrooms: **2**. Room rate from: **£65**

Fore Street, Milverton, near Taunton, Somerset, TA4 1JX.
T: 01823 400534

www.theglobemilverton.co.uk

The Globe Milverton
@infomilverton

TRENCHERMAN'S COLLECTIONS

Take five for decadent glamour

19 Harvey Nichols Second Floor Restaurant
Did we mention the gold leather banquettes, classy cooking and very smart service?

60 Gidleigh Park
New head chef Michael Wignall brings his precise, contemporary cooking to the oak panelled, decadent Dartmoor retreat.

8 Lucknam Park Hotel and Spa
Rejuvenate in the über glam spa, before donning your best threads for a fabulous dining experience.

1 The Slaughters Manor House
Fine dining and sumptuous bedrooms provide plenty of scope for playing at being lord and lady of the manor for the evening.

110 The Idle Rocks
Coastal chic, done in impeccable style makes this boutique hotel which overlooking St Mawes harbour, a stunning spot for dinner and drinks.

DORSET & HAMPSHIRE

Captain's Club Hotel and Spa **No. 51**

43 Riverside Restaurant
44 Best Western The Grange at Oborne
45 The Three Lions
46 HIX Oyster and Fish House
47 Crab House Cafe
48 The Acorn Inn
49 The Fontmell
50 WestBeach
51 Captain's Club Hotel and Spa

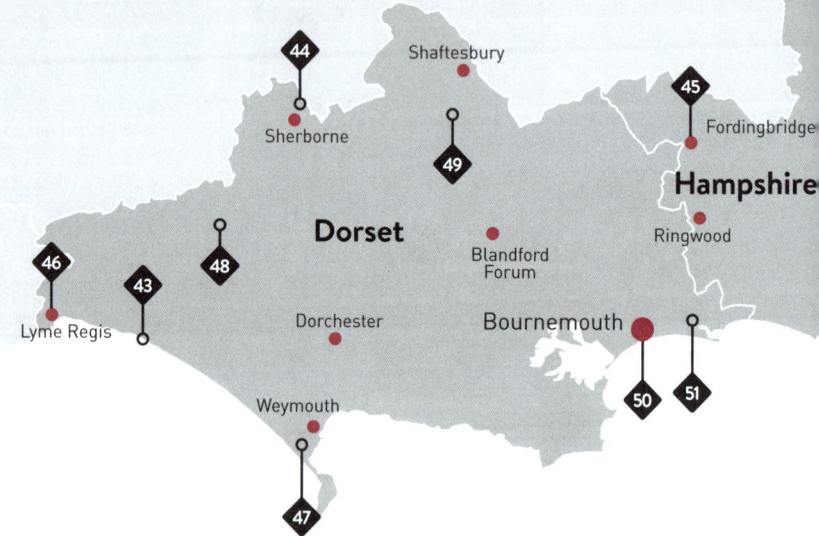

Restaurants listed in the guide correspond to the numbers plotted on the map. Locations are approximate.

New restaurants to the guide are highlighted in red.

43
Riverside Restaurant

SUBLIME SEAFOOD AT A MUCH LOVED RESTAURANT

For somewhere special to eat seafood in Dorset there's one place that needs to go to the top of any wish-list, and that's Riverside Restaurant in West Bay, Bridport.

It enjoys a prime location, with large picture windows overlooking the River Brit, but that's just one element of the charm of this long established restaurant. It's also a pioneer in its use of local produce to create truly special fish and shellfish dishes – along with alternative meat and vegetarian options which change by the day.

Call in for a light snack, a midweek great value lunch or plump for a leisurely evening seafood feast and match it with something very satisfying from an impressive wine list, with plenty of great choices under £20. An à la carte menu is also available.

Chef: **Tony Shaw**
3 course lunch from: **£29**
3 course dinner from: **£35**
Seats: **80, private room up to 30**

West Bay, Bridport, Dorset, DT6 4EZ.
T: 01308 422011

www.thefishrestaurant-westbay.co.uk

- Riverside Restaurant
- @riversidewb

44
Best Western The Grange at Oborne

ELEGANT DORSET DINING RETREAT

Reflecting the mellow tones of the Purbeck stone which is everywhere in the pretty West Dorset village of Oborne, The Grange has a timeless quality.

Privately owned and family run, its origins date back 200 years. Nowadays head chef Simon Clewlow leads the kitchen with his modern English menus making full use of the local and seasonal produce.

The restaurant overlooks the gardens which are a perfect place to sit in the afternoon sun. And with 18 comfortable bedrooms there's ample reason to linger over a candlelit meal and enjoy the magical scene when they become floodlit at night.

The Grange holds a good clutch of awards and in 2015 added a gold Taste of the West and Dorset Tourism's Small Hotel of Year title.

Chef: **Simon Clewlow**
3 course lunch from: **£26**
3 course dinner from: **£35**
Seats: **45**
Bedrooms: **18**
Room rate from: **£99**

Oborne, Sherborne, Dorset, DT9 4LA.
T: 01935 813463

www.thegrangeatoborne.co.uk

- The Grange at Oborne
- @grangeatoborne
- @grangeatoborne

45 ⑤
The Three Lions

EXCEPTIONAL BRITISH/FRENCH COOKING FROM ACCLAIMED CHEF

Not only is this a multi-award winning restaurant with rooms – named Hampshire Restaurant of the Year three times - it's also got an impressive guest list of famous customers, from politicians to royalty.

Family-run for the past 21 years, head chef Mike Womersley (who held a star for five years at Lucknam Park) is the main man in the kitchen and creates an exceptional menu of classical British/French dishes.

Everything is made in-house and ingredients treated with the utmost respect, as you'd expect of a chef of this calibre. Inside it's cosy with a log burning fire and conservatory meeting room, while there are also gardens, a sauna and whirlpool to tempt you to stay the night.

Chef: **Mike Womersley**
3 course lunch from: **£23.50**
3 course dinner from: **£29.50**
Seats: **60**
Bedrooms: **7**
Room rate from: **£125**

Stuckton, Fordingbridge, Hampshire, SP6 2HF.
T: 01425 652489

www.thethreelionsrestaurant.com

TRENCHERMAN'S COLLECTIONS

Take five for a cosy getaway

81 The NoBody Inn
This ancient inn near Exeter, is just the place to escape to the countryside for great food, cosy nooks and a seriously great wine and whisky list with over 300 to explore.

95 Q Restaurant at The Old Quay House Hotel
Sporting a glam refurb, this smart little hotel in yachty Fowey has a magical terrace for a waterside aperitif as the sun goes down.

73 Cary Arms
Rural pub meets boutique hotel that's cosy in winter and seasidey in summer. Book the Captain's Table for the best seat in the house.

4 The Miners Country Inn
Escape to the Forest of Dean for country walks, pints in the bar and seriously good cooking at this relaxed foodie local with rooms.

6 The Bell at Ramsbury
This elegant Wiltshire inn ticks all the boxes: rustic charm, stylish bedrooms, roaring fire and modern British cooking using produce sourced from its own garden.

DORSET & HAMPSHIRE

46
HIX Oyster and Fish House

Chef Mark Hix is in his native element in Dorset and revels in letting the local seafood and foraged produce do the talking on his daily-changing menus.

The backdrop to this pleasingly simple but beautifully executed cooking is an informal, airy dining room with simple furniture that provides diners with stunning panoramic views across the Jurassic coast and Lyme Regis.

In warmer months, the sun terrace is the hot place to soak up the views and sample seasonal cocktails.

Chef: **Charlie Soole**. 3 courses lunch from: **£21** 3 course dinner from: **£35**. Seats: **42**

Cobb Road, Lyme Regis, Dorset, DT7 3JP.
T: 01297 446910

www.hixoysterandfishhouse.co.uk

- HIX Restaurants
- @hixrestaurants
- @hixrestaurants

47
Crab House Cafe

If the name hasn't already given it away, seafood is the star of show at this award-winning beachside eatery. With fish landed at Weymouth, Poole and Brixham coming into the kitchen throughout the day, expect a menu of piscatorial delights that changes by the hour.

Chef patron Nigel Bloxham grows the accompanying herbs for the flavoursome dishes, and there's a veg patch right alongside the shack giving new meaning to hyperlocal. Make sure to try the oysters, they're hauled right outside the cafe from their own oyster farm.

Chef: **Nigel Bloxham**. 3 course lunch from: **£25**. 3 course dinner from: **£25**. Seats: **48**

The Fleet Oyster Farm, Ferrymans Way, Portland Road, Wyke Regis, Dorset, DT4 9YU.
T: 01305 788867

www.crabhousecafe.co.uk

- Crab House
- @crabhousecafe

48
The Acorn Inn

This Grade I-listed 16th century coaching inn is as popular with the locals as it is with visitors. Inside it's atmospheric and welcoming with original oak panelling and flagstone floors and there's a tempting array of real ales, ciders and more than 100 single malt whiskies to choose from. Menus draw on ingredients from local farmers and suppliers. It amply deserves its gold in the Taste of the West awards.

Chefs: **Guy Horley and Jack Mackenzie**.
3 course lunch from: **£25**. 3 course dinner from: **£25**. Seats: **40**. Bedrooms: **10**. Room rate from: **£99 (double)**

28 Fore Street, Evershot, Dorset, DT2 0JW.

T: 01935 83228

www.acorn-inn.co.uk

- The Acorn Inn
- @acorn-inn
- @acorn_inn

49
The Fontmell

A stunning renovation of this country pub has included extending the building over the Collier's Brook stream, which now flows between the bar and the dining room. It's created a magical atmosphere, especially when the windows are open on a warm summer's evening and the sound of the water mingles with the hum of conversation. Menus are equally distinctive, with a refreshing fusion of cuisines created by chef Tom Shaw.

Chef: **Tom Shaw**. 3 course lunch from: **£25**. 3 course dinner from: **£25**. Seats: **60**. Bedrooms: **6**. Room rate from: **£75**

Crown Hill, Fontmell Magna, Shaftesbury, Dorset, SP7 0PA.

T: 01747 811441

www.thefontmell.com

- The Fontmell
- @thefontmell
- @thefontmell

50
WestBeach

No visit to Bournemouth is complete without popping in to this contemporary seafood restaurant which is right next to the beach by the town's famous pier.

Seafood used on the menu is caught by the restaurant's own fishing boats and prepared with other carefully sourced local ingredients. And when you've finished being entranced by the expansive beach views, you can watch the chefs at work in the open plan kitchen. Wines are a speciality too, so enjoy a glass sitting on the sunny terrace.

Chef: **Marcin Pacholarz**. 3 course lunch from: **£30**. 3 course dinner from: **£32**. Seats: **75**

Pier Approach, Bournemouth, Dorset, BH2 5AA.

T: 01202 587785

www.west-beach.co.uk

- WestBeach
- @westbeachbmouth
- @westbeachbmouth

51
Captain's Club Hotel and Spa

There's no better way to arrive at this striking waterfront hotel and spa than by boat, but even if you don't make an entrance by water, you can still enjoy the modern take on the maritime theme that pervades this four star establishment.

On the banks of the River Stour, just a short stroll from the historic market town of Christchurch, this is a great place for all day dining. Eat on the fab terrace, or in the restaurant which has its own cocktail bar and waterfall feature for a truly unique atmosphere.

Chef: **Andrew Gault**. 3 course lunch from: **£25**. 3 course dinner from: **£25**. Seats: **100**. Bedrooms: **29**. Room rate from: **£179**

Wick Ferry, Christchurch, Dorset, BH23 1HU.

T: 01202 475111

www.captainsclubhotel.com

- Captains Club Hotel and Spa
- @theofficialcch
- @captainsclubhotel

DEVON

Hotel Endsleigh **No. 63**

- **52** Saunton Sands Hotel
- **53** Watersmeet Hotel
- **54** The Coach House by Michael Caines
- **55** The Masons Arms
- **56** The Swan
- **57** The Salty Monk Restaurant with Rooms
- **58** The Riviera Hotel and Restaurant
- **59** ABode Exeter
- **60** Gidleigh Park
- **61** Lewtrenchard Manor
- **62** The Arundell Arms Hotel and Restaurant
- **63** Hotel Endsleigh
- **64** The Horn of Plenty
- **65** Two Bridges Hotel
- **66** Prince Hall Hotel and Restaurant
- **67** Rock Salt Cafe
- **68** The Greedy Goose
- **69** The Treby Arms
- **70** Plantation House Hotel and Restaurant
- **71** Glazebrook House Hotel
- **72** Soar Mill Cove Hotel and Spa
- **73** Cary Arms
- **74** The (Exmoor) Beastro
- **75** The Hartnoll Hotel
- **76** The Lazy Toad Inn
- **77** The Rusty Bike
- **78** The Salutation Inn
- **79** The Galley Restaurant
- **80** Rodean Restaurant
- **81** The NoBody Inn
- **82** The Horse
- **83** Ilsington Country House Hotel and Spa
- **84** The Cornish Arms
- **85** Barbican Kitchen
- **86** Langdon Court Restaurant
- **87** Boringdon Hall
- **88** The Millbrook Inn
- **89** The Grill Room
- **90** Royal Seven Stars Hotel
- **91** Dartington Hall
- **92** The Orange Tree Restaurant

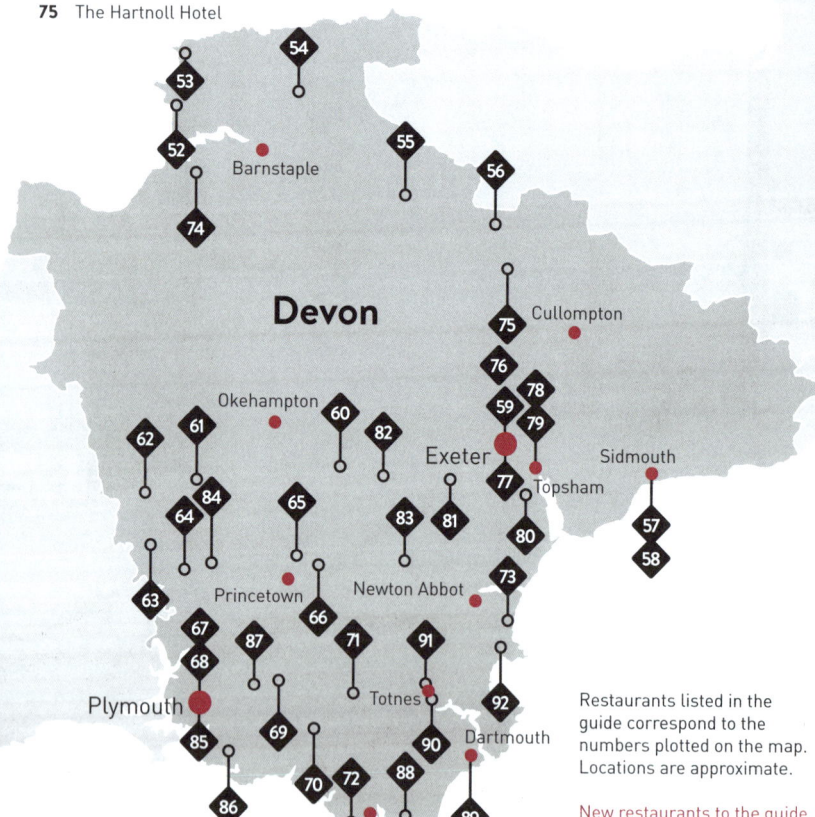

Restaurants listed in the guide correspond to the numbers plotted on the map. Locations are approximate.

New restaurants to the guide are highlighted in red.

52
Saunton Sands Hotel

WORLD CLASS VIEWS MAKE AN EXPERIENCE TO REMEMBER

With possibly the most stunning views in the South West, lunch or dinner in the Terrace Restaurant at Saunton Sands Hotel is an experience to remember.

When the weather's cooler, dine in the smartly refurbished art deco restaurant that echoes the stylistic sensibilities of this family friendly hotel on the north Devon coast.

Head chef Jamie Coleman (who featured this year on *BBC Masterchef: The Professionals*) creates modern dishes that celebrate the seasons, and this style and comfort is echoed in the hotel's lovely décor and smart service.

Chef: **Jamie Coleman**
3 course lunch from: **£19.95**
4 course dinner from: **£38**
Seats: **150**
Bedrooms: **83**
Room rate from: **£90**

Saunton, near Braunton, Devon, EX33 1LQ.
T: 01271 890212

www.sauntonsands.co.uk

- Saunton Sands Hotel
- @sauntonsandshot
- @saunton_sandshotel

53
Watersmeet Hotel

AIRY COASTAL DINING

In a fabulous position overlooking what's officially been named the UK's Best Beach for the second year running, this year's guests at Watersmeet can get even closer to Woolacombe's rolling breakers, thanks to the hotel's new terrace.

If the weather's good you'd be daft not to dine outdoors, while the circular Pavilion Restaurant with two AA rosettes for smart cooking, also has panoramic views of the dazzling coastline.

The charming boutique hotel embodies the spirit of great British seaside holidays, while providing chic, airy decor with a touch of New England style. Visit for a champagne afternoon tea or lunch at the hotel's informal bistro.

Chef: **John Prince**
3 course lunch from: **£25**
3 course dinner from: **£45**
Seats: **60**
Bedrooms: **29**
Room rate from: **£95**

Woolacombe, Devon, EX34 7EB.
T: 01271 870333

www.watersmeethotel.co.uk

- Watersmeet Hotel
- @watersmeethotel
- @watersmeetwoolacombe

54 $

The Coach House by Michael Caines

THE CAINES' TOUCH COMES TO NORTH DEVON

Since leaving ABode to focus on other projects Michael Caines has cherry picked some key restaurants to be intimately involved with, and one such establishment is The Coach House.

With his protégé, the talented Thomas Hine at the helm, the restaurant is bringing the MC experience to this attractive converted 17th century coach house on the edge of Exmoor. Expect modern European cuisine, with Caines' trademark elegant simplicity running throughout – nothing's on the plate that doesn't add something significant – alongside a pleasing wine selection.

Chef: **Thomas Hine**
3 course lunch from: **£24.95**
3 course dinner from: **£45**
Seats: **50**
Bedrooms: **16**
Room rate from: **£125**

Kentisbury Grange, Kentisbury, Barnstaple, Devon, EX31 4NL.
T: 01271 882295

www.kentisburygrange.com

- Kentisbury Grange
- @kgcoachhouse
- @kentisburygrange

55

The Masons Arms

MICHELIN ACHIEVEMENT IN A VILLAGE PUB SETTING

When Mark Dodson, (ex head chef at Michel Roux's Waterside Inn in Bray), and wife Sarah arrived in north Devon ten years ago with an aim of creating a fine dining pub restaurant, no doubt the locals thought this might be another flash in the pan. However, a decade on, and the pair are celebrating the huge achievement of holding a Michelin star at The Masons Arms for ten years, alongside being voted number 10 in this year's UK's Top 50 Gastropubs. It's not surprising, given the high quality of British and French cuisine being served, and with an unpretentious attitude and cosy bar to boot, they've kept the locals as well as the gourmet tourists happy.

Chef: **Mark Dodson**
3 course lunch from: **£25**
3 course dinner from: **£40**
Seats: **28**

Knowstone, South Molton, Devon, EX36 4RY.
T: 01398 341231

www.masonsarmsdevon.co.uk

- The Masons Arms Knowstone
- @masonsknowstone

56
The Swan

WISH-IT-WAS-YOUR-LOCAL DINING PUB

It's been an extraordinary year for Paul and Donna Berry at The Swan in Bampton. Not only did the cheffing duo take home the Best Pub accolade at the 2016 Trencherman's Awards, but they've added a whole host of regional and national silverware to the 15th century village pub's mantelpiece. It's easy to see why the couple have done so well, working tirelessly to create an inspiring line-up

BEST PUB 2016

of innovative classic British dishes, with stunning produce sourced from the surrounding Devon countryside. There's a warm and welcoming atmosphere to be found at The Swan, with locals popping in for a pint and visitors making the journey for the impressive fare and a night above the inn.

Chefs: **Paul and Donna Berry**
3 course set lunch: **£20**
3 course dinner from: **£25**
Seats: **58**
Bedrooms: **3**
Room rate from: **£85**

Station Road, Bampton, Tiverton, Devon, EX16 9NG.
T: 01398 332248

www.theswan.co

The Swan   @theswanbampton   @theswanbampton

57

The Salty Monk Restaurant with Rooms

BEAUTIFULLY CRAFTED IN SIDMOUTH

Quietly turning out some of the best food the region has to offer, Andy Witheridge is highly respected by his peers – and a visit to The Salty Monk reveals why.

Andy's skill and meticulous flair is unquestionable and the years at his own restaurant have seen his individual culinary style flourish. Diners can experience this at The Salty Monk's relaxed Abbots Den Brasserie or plump for fine dining in the Garden Room restaurant - both are modern and comfortable inside.

And when Andy's not in the kitchen, you'll probably find him tutoring chefs of the future – such is his passion for good food.

Chefs: **Andy Witheridge and Scott Horn**
3 course lunch from: **£24**
3 course dinner from: **£35**
Seats: **30**
Bedrooms: **6**
Room rate from: **£130**

Church Street, Sidford, Sidmouth, Devon, EX10 9QP.
T: 01395 513174

www.saltymonk.co.uk

The Salty Monk Restaurant With Rooms
@saltymonk

58

The Riviera Hotel and Restaurant

THE CLASSIC RIVIERA EXPERIENCE

For grandeur by the sea and two AA rosette dining, head to Sidmouth where you'll easily spot the elegant Riviera Hotel on the coastal town's Esplanade.

Inside, there's an impressive choice to be found on chef Martin Osedo's menus, and each dish is created with an attention to detail that's echoed throughout the hotel.

Run by the same family for more than 40 years, the generational theme extends to the menus with fish sourced from a third generation family fishing business. Enjoy cocktails in the Regency Bar or lunch on the terrace for the full riviera-chic experience.

Chef: **Martin Osedo**
2 course lunch: **£26**
4 course lunch: **£29.50**
3 course dinner: **£39**
5 course dinner: **£43**
Seats: **80 in restaurant, 60 on terrace**
Bedrooms: **26**
Room rate from: **£109**

The Esplanade, Sidmouth, Devon, EX10 8AY.
T: 01395 515201

www.hotelriviera.co.uk

59
ABode Exeter

SMART DINING, SERVED WITH STYLE

A stay at ABode Exeter is to experience the charm of this historic city, with all the mod cons and luxury you'd expect from a top end hotel.

One of the great attractions is the stunning view of the cathedral which is just a stone's throw across the green from this 300-year-old hotel (said to be Britain's oldest). Then there's the intimate champagne bar, airy restaurant and, of course, modern British cuisine created by head chef Alex Gibbs and team.

The tasting menu is especially fabulous, and served with aplomb by an international team of hospitality professionals.

Chef: **Alex Gibbs**
3 course lunch from: **£22**
3 course dinner from: **£25**
Seats: **60**
Bedrooms: **53**
Room rate from: **£99**

Cathedral Yard, Exeter, Devon, EX1 1HD.
T: 01392 319955

www.abodeexeter.co.uk

ABode Hotels
@abodeexeter

TRENCHERMAN'S COLLECTIONS

Take five glorious afternoon teas

21 **The Bath Priory**
Summer in the city? Indulge in an exquisite tea on the flower-filled terrace at the Michelin starred restaurant and hotel.

65 **Two Bridges Hotel**
Take a wild walk on Dartmoor in winter before bagging a spot by one of the many roaring fires for a tea that's groaning with goodies.

53 **Watersmeet Hotel**
Raise a glass of fizz to Britain's best beach at north Devon's airy, contemporary take on the traditional British seaside hotel.

111 **The Water's Edge**
One for the savoury toothed is the Gentleman's Tea of scotch quail's eggs, steak and stilton sandwiches, cheese, beer and bacon scones, chocolate stout cake and more at Falmouth's The Greenbank Hotel.

7 **The Pear Tree at Purton**
Take tea on the terrace of the seven acre garden and wildflower meadow, with a glass of Cuvee Anne, created at the hotel's vineyard.

60 ⓢ
Gidleigh Park

NEW DIRECTION FOR IMPECCABLE HOTEL

One of the South West's most exquisite dining experiences, this year sees Gidleigh take a fresh culinary direction as a result of the appointment of new executive head chef, Michael Wignall (ex of Pennyhill Park in Surrey).

Famed for his precise cooking and respect for ingredients, Michael's lead is unique dishes with the emphasis on flavour, underpinned by a contemporary, more informal approach.

In addition to superb food, it's the impeccable service and extensive wine list (the cellar holds 13,000 bottles) which are the star attractions at this quietly glamorous Tudor-style house set in 107 acres on romantic Dartmoor.

Chef: **Michael Wignall**
3 course lunch from: **£40**
7 course tasting menu: **£110**
Seats: **52**
Bedrooms: **24**
Room rate from: **£250**

Chagford, Devon, TQ13 8HH.
T: 01647 432367

www.gidleigh.co.uk

 Gidleigh Park
@gidleighhotel

61 ⓢ
Lewtrenchard Manor

CONTEMPORARY COOKING IN A HISTORIC SETTING

A stunning Jacobean manor house, Lewtenchard is owned by the Murray family, and retains a family feel despite its impressive historical credentials.

In the kitchen, experienced head chef Matthew Peryer creates vibrant and meticulous dishes and guests can watch the team at work by dining at the Purple Carrot chef's table. Matthew's menus make full use of local produce and the manor's own restored and productive kitchen garden.

Inside, you'll find wood panelled rooms and a fabulous carved fireplace but during the summer months make the most of the Italianate courtyard with wisteria-lined walls.

Chef: **Matthew Peryer**
3 course lunch from: **£24**
3 course dinner from: **£49.50**
Seats: **40**
Bedrooms: **14**
Room rate from: **£165**

Lewdown, Okehampton, Devon, EX20 4PN.
T: 01566 783222

www.lewtrenchard.co.uk

 Lewtrenchard Manor
@lewtrenchard

62

The Arundell Arms Hotel and Restaurant

REELING IN THE REGULARS

A country retreat in every sense of the word, the Arundell Arms is a winning mix of country pub, fine dining restaurant and fishing lodge that's been owned by the same family for over 50 years.

The kitchen is led by Master Chef Steve Pidgeon whose unfailing commitment to unearthing the best local ingredients and turning them into very special dishes, won him Food magazine's Best Chef 2016.

The setting in a valley close to the uplands of Dartmoor is delightful too, and guests can make full use of it by enjoying country sports such as fly fishing, for which the Arundell Arms is known and loved.

Chef: **Steve Pidgeon**
3 course lunch from: **£23**
3 course dinner from: **£35**
Seats: **80**
Bedrooms: **27**
Room rate from: **£95**

Fore Street, Lifton, Devon, PL16 0AA.
T: 01566 784666

www.arundellarms.com

- The Arundell Arms Hotel
- @thearundellarms

63

Hotel Endsleigh

STUNNING COUNTRY HOUSE HOTEL

There's some seriously impressive seasonal fare to be sampled at Hotel Endsleigh near Tavistock.

Head chef Jose Graziosi, formerly of The Seafood Restaurant, took over the kitchen in May 2015 and has been busy creating a stunning repertoire of fine dining dishes inspired by both his Italian homeland and the local Devon produce.

There's more than simply fine food to be found at this country house hotel though, and the delights include quirky country house décor, first-rate service from general manager Adam Cornish and team, 18 lavish boudoirs and 108 acres of beautiful gardens (with historic shell house) that are waiting to be explored.

Chef: **Jose Graziosi**
3 course lunch from: **£26**
3 course dinner from: **£44**
Seats: **45**
Bedrooms: **18**
Room rate from: **£190**

Milton Abbot, Tavistock, Devon, PL19 0PQ.
T: 01822 870000

www.hotelendsleigh.com

- Hotel Endsleigh
- @hotelendsleigh
- @hotelendsleigh

64

The Horn of Plenty

POLISH AND PEDIGREE

Upholding its renowned culinary pedigree, this country house close to Tavistock continues to serve an immaculate food offering.

The team's skilful use of ingredients, an incredible 90 per cent of which come from the South West, means dishes are seasonal and inspiring.

A collection of chic bedrooms – some in the old house, some in the modern Coach House extension, have views over the Tamar Valley and grounds, including a beautiful walled garden. All of this means there's ample excuse to extend your stay and sample the superb breakfasts before heading off.

3 course lunch from: **£24.50**
3 course dinner from: **£49.50**
Seats: **50**
Bedrooms: **16**
Room rate from: **£110**

Gulworthy, Tavistock, Devon, PL19 8JD.
T: 01822 832528

www.thehornofplenty.co.uk

The Horn of Plenty Country House Hotel & Restaurant
@hornofplenty1

INSIDER'S TIP

'With Michael Wignall's arrival at Gidleigh Park (No. 60), it's definitely the restaurant at the top of my to-visit list.'

Matthew Peryer, head chef, Lewtrenchard Manor **No. 61**

65

Two Bridges Hotel

DARTMOOR'S GREAT ESCAPE

With executive chef Mike Palmer at the helm, this historic Dartmoor hotel can boast a superb food offering. Perfectly placed for exploring the surrounding stunning moorland, Two Bridges is a welcoming stop off point for fabulous lunches and very decadent afternoon teas.

Its sofa-filled, double fireplace entrance sets the scene for comfort, relaxation and a pre-dinner drink. Then find a window spot in the Tors restaurant and enjoy the views over the riverside setting. Its chef's selection of local and regional produce is top notch and detailed – from Dartmoor lamb and beef right through to the jams on the breakfast table. Frequent special events also showcase the team's culinary expertise.

Chef: **Mike Palmer**
3 course lunch from: **£22**
3 course dinner from: **£37.50**
Seats: **60**
Bedrooms: **32**
Room rate from: **£90**

Two Bridges, Yelverton, Devon, PL20 6SW.
T: 01822 892300

www.twobridges.co.uk
- Two Bridges Hotel
- @two_bridges

66

Prince Hall Hotel and Restaurant

CHARMING RETREAT ON DARTMOOR

A beech tree drive leads to this jewel of a hotel deep in the heart of Dartmoor. It's where Fi and Chris Daly charm visitors with a combination of beautifully accomplished cooking and home-from-home atmosphere.

With just eight rooms, it's a perfect retreat and before dining there's an opportunity to relax in the lounge with an aperitif and read up on Prince Hall's rich and characterful history.

Perfect for walkers and those exploring Dartmoor, the moor is, literally, a step away. It's extremely dog friendly too; four legged friends are as welcome as their owners, and there's a dog-friendly dining area. Also pop in for lunch on the lawn or an excellent cream tea with scones warm from the oven.

Chef: **Chris Daly**
2 course light lunch from: **£17.50**
3 course lunch from: **£24.95**
3 course dinner from: **£47.50**
Seats: **20**
Bedrooms: **8**
Room rate from: **£160**

Near Princetown, Yelverton, Devon, PL20 6SA.
T: 01822 890403

www.princehall.co.uk
- Prince Hall Hotel & Restaurant
- @princehallhotel

67
Rock Salt Cafe

A DASH OF ASIAN INFLUENCE

In the last year, Rock Salt Cafe has notched up further awards including two AA rosettes, which is a well deserved coup for this unassuming little family run brasserie, close to the ferry port in the Millbay area of Plymouth.

Chef David Jenkins has become a local legend, drawing diners from near and far for his imaginative dishes, with an exciting dash of Asian influence.

True to its ethos of being a relaxed place to enjoy good, honest food, you're as welcome to pop in for cake and coffee or an all day breakfast as you are to linger over a brasserie style evening meal which reveals chef's fine dining credentials. Check out its new (and nearby) sister pub restaurant, Salumi, too.

Chef: **David Jenkins**
3 course lunch from: **£18**
3 course dinner from: **£22**
Seats: **70**

31 Stonehouse Street, Plymouth, Devon, PL1 3PE.
T: 01752 225522

www.rocksaltcafe.co.uk

- Rock Salt Cafe Brasserie
- @rocksaltcafeuk
- @rocksaltcafe

68
The Greedy Goose

FABULOUS FINE DINING IN PLYMOUTH

Experienced head chef Ben Palmer and partner Francesca are serving up authentic, modern British cooking in style at Plymouth's historic Prysten House.

It's a great destination for an excellent value special lunch menu, but to really see what this chef can do, we'd recommend plumping for the fine dining, à la carte menu where beautifully prepared dishes are playful and entertaining. Service is friendly and attentive and the matched 'mostly red' or 'mostly white' wine flights are a pleasing touch.

Chef: **Ben Palmer**
3 course lunch from: **£12**
3 course dinner from: **£12**
Seats: **40**

Prysten House, Finewell Street, Plymouth, Devon, PL1 2AE.
T: 01752 252001

www.thegreedygoose.co.uk

- The Greedy Goose
- @greedygooseplym
- @greedygooseplym

69
The Treby Arms

FOOD AS THEATRE IN A DEVON DINING PUB

Chef patron Anton Piotrowski and his team took the gong for Best Restaurant at the 2015 Trencherman's Awards, which is just one of the many trophies (including a Michelin star) which have been awarded to this creative chef.

This dining pub near Plymouth is Anton's main HQ and while the cosy downstairs bar is all log fires and locals imbibing real ales, the first floor dining room is where the magic is revealed.

It's a setting for some excitingly experimental "food as theatre" experiences. And with friendly, assured service and playful presentation, this is dining to savour - and remember.

Chef: **Anton Piotrowski**
3 course lunch from: **£23**
3 course dinner from: **£43**
Seats: **60**

6 Newtons Row, Sparkwell, Plympton, Devon, PL7 5DD.
T: 01752 837363

www.thetrebyarms.co.uk

Treby Arms
@thetrebyarms

70 $

Plantation House Hotel and Restaurant

A FOODIE HOME FROM HOME

Set in a picture perfect Devon valley, the Plantation House is a privately owned, boutique hotel and restaurant which has been sensitively and stylishly restored.

This a home from home – with luxurious extras such as under-floor heated bathrooms and bedroom sound systems.

Everything served in the restaurant is prepared in-house, from bread to patisserie and chocolates, by chefs Richard Hendey and John Raines. Expect bold and exciting dishes using veg grown in the kitchen garden, fish from the nearby river and sea, and foraged goodies from the wild and beautiful surrounding countryside.

Chefs: **Richard Hendey and John Raines**
5 course dinner from: **£36**
Seats: **26**
Bedrooms: **7**
Room rate from: **£110**

Totnes Road, Ermington, Ivybridge, Devon, PL21 9NS.
T: 01548 831100

www.plantationhousehotel.co.uk

71

Glazebrook House Hotel

QUIRKY GLAMOUR AND A PREMIER CHEF AT BOUTIQUE HOTEL

Through the collaboration of Glazebrook's creative team and interior designer Timothy Oulton, this luxurious boutique hotel is both chic and enchanting.

Stunning British revival décor, sumptuous handmade furnishings and beguiling vintage curios are equalled by the creative menu devised by the hotel's new executive chef Anton Piotrowski (Michelin starred and *BBC Masterchef: The Professionals* winner). His talented team takes the very best local and seasonal produce to create exciting dishes which are served in a quirky, glamorous dining room.

Chef: **Anton Piotrowski**
3 course lunch from: **£19.95**
3 course dinner from: **£32**
Seats: **40**
Bedrooms: **8**
Room rate from: **£199**

Glazebrook, South Brent, Devon, TQ10 9JE.
T: 01364 73322

www.glazebrookhouse.com

Glazebrook House Hotel
@glazebrookhouse

TRENCHERMAN'S COLLECTIONS

Take five for foodie families

106 Zacry's at Watergate Bay Hotel
Take the kids to this funky, family-friendly hotel for American style dining at Zacry's restaurant and fun activities for youngsters.

103 The Cornish Arms
Stein's country pub is the perfect stop off after a day on the beach. Lots of space, real ales, great home cooking and classics like scampi in a basket will keep everyone happy.

52 Saunton Sands Hotel
After a day running around the dunes, eat together on the fabulous terrace, or if you stay kids can have their own early high tea.

102 Rick Stein's Cafe
Relaxed and beachy, it's an easy place to take kids for palate-expanding, pan-global cooking. Happily, there's also a kids' menu for fussy eaters.

85 Barbican Kitchen
A buzzy, contemporary brasserie in the Plymouth Gin Distillery, the Tanner brothers' restaurant is so family friendly that kids under five eat free.

72
Soar Mill Cove Hotel and Spa

ESCAPE TO A MAGICAL COVE

A luxurious retreat at the end of a Devon lane and a few steps from a magical cove, being at Soar Mill feels truly remote, even though it's only a short distance from the buzzing streets of yachty Salcombe.

In the same family for three generations and impressively retaining many key members of staff, there's a genuine welcoming family feel.

TRENCHERMAN'S AWARDS
BEST DINE AND STAY EXPERIENCE
2016

Tradition hasn't held back development though, so elements such as its spa credentials are top notch – try a pamper break or a dip and dine spa day.

Chef Ian Macdonald has gathered an impressive list of local suppliers so you can sample the best of the South Hams including Salcombe crab and Start Bay scallops.

Chef: **Ian Macdonald**.
3 course set lunch: **£23**
3 course dinner from: **£35**
Seats: **60**
Bedrooms: **22**
Room rate from: **£159**

Malborough, near Salcombe, Devon, TQ7 3DS.
T: 01548 561566

www.soarmillcove.co.uk

 Soar Mill Cove Hotel    @soarmillcove   @soarmillcovehotel

73

Cary Arms

BOUTIQUE SEASIDE HOTEL

Perched above Babbacombe Bay, the Cary Arms is a seaside hotel that's decidedly different.

Blending the best bits of the country inn experience (crackling log fires, local ales and comfy atmosphere) with the glamour of a boutique break (sleek suites and quirky touches), it's no wonder the "inn and spa on the beach" is a popular spot for a great British getaway.

Head chef Ben Kingdon has the dining element covered with a pleasing mix of classics such as West Country steak and chips, and fine dining dishes including pan seared pigeon breast. There are also regular gourmet events including tasting evenings and one-off gastro menus, to provide a real taste of the Cary.

Chef: **Ben Kingdon**
3 course lunch from: **£25**
3 course dinner from: **£30**
Seats: **65**
Bedrooms: **18 rooms and 2 cottages**
Room rate from: **£195**

Babbacombe Beach, Babbacombe, Devon, TQ1 3LX.
T: 01803 327110

www.caryarms.co.uk

- The Cary Arms
- @caryarms
- @caryarms

INSIDER'S TIP

'One of my favourite restaurants is Casamia (No. 20) in Bristol. The cooking is exceptional, so you need to book well in advance to get a table.'

Chris Cleghorn, head chef, The Olive Tree **No. 24**

DEVON

74
The (Exmoor) Beastro

Prepare for something different from Alex Nutt and Fiona O'Mahoney, who are at their happiest cooking directly over a wood fire. Back to basics, yes, but the way these skilled chefs play with flavours and are inspired by world cuisines, produces extraordinary results. The Beastro's move from Dulverton to Tapeley Park, with its strong organic credentials, permaculture garden and grass fed Highland cattle, is a perfect fit. And being housed in the estate's elegant Queen Anne Dairy provides a suitably creative setting to watch these innovative cooks perform.

Chefs: **Alexander Nutt and Fiona O'Mahoney**. 3 course lunch from: **£20**. 3 course dinner from: **£35**. Seats: **40-80**

Tapeley Park Estate and Gardens, Instow, Devon, EX39 4NT.
T: 01271 861796

www.beastro.uk

- The Exmoor Beastro
- @exmoorbeast
- @the_exmoor_beast

75
The Hartnoll Hotel

Get stuck into the Exmoor experience at this little boutique hotel across the way from National Trust property Knightshayes near Tiverton.

Head chef Boyd Snelling's menus are relaxed and crowd pleasing, with good steaks and chops to be had on the grill menu too. It's popular with the hunting, shooting and fishing set who, understandably, like to eat out on the attractive garden terrace in summer.

Chef: **Boyd Snelling**. 3 course lunch from: **£20**. 3 course dinner from: **£30**. Seats: **120**. Bedrooms: **18**. Room rate from: **£75**

Bolham, Tiverton, Devon, EX16 7RA.
T: 01884 252777

www.hartnollhotel.co.uk

- Hartnoll Hotel
- @hartnollhotel

76
The Lazy Toad Inn

With its pretty blue framed windows, this Grade II-listed pub in the charming village of Brampford Speke in the Exe Valley is one of those spots where you'll want to while away more than a few hours.

Grab a moment in the sun in the cobbled courtyard then head inside, where slate floors, oak beamed ceilings and a great selection of locally made real ales, ciders and wines are very appealing. The food is excellent with new head chef Steve Mabbutt making best use of veg, fruit and herbs from the inn's own smallholding.

Chef: **Steve Mabbutt**. 3 course lunch from: **£22**. 3 course dinner from: **£25**. Seats: **65**.

Brampford Speke, Exeter, Devon, EX5 5DP.

T: 01392 841591

www.thelazytoadinn.com

- The Lazy Toad Inn
- @thelazytoadinn

78
The Salutation Inn

Tom Williams-Hawkes was a finalist in the Best Chef category of the Trencherman's Awards 2015, and clearly delights diners at his Topsham restaurant. Using fresh fish from the River Exe and local seafood, Tom's accomplished cooking is set off by the striking glass atrium restaurant at the 18th century building. Warm service led by Amelia Boalch, a comfortable lounge and bedrooms, plus private dining complete the package.

Chef: **Tom Williams-Hawkes**. Lunch from: **£8.50**. 4 course dinner from: **£39.50**. Seats: **28**. Bedrooms: **6**. Room rate from: **£135**

68 Fore Street, Topsham, Devon, EX3 0HL.

T: 01392 873060

www.salutationtopsham.co.uk

- Salutation Inn
- @salutation1
- @thesalutationinn

77
The Rusty Bike

Tucked away in a quiet street behind Exeter's historic prison, The Rusty Bike is a back-street boozer worth the detour. It's a place to hunker down with friends for the afternoon around a well-loved wooden table upon wonky wooden benches. Not only does this characterful pub harbour an attractive line-up of real ales (from its own Fat Pig brewery), exotic spirits and wines, there's also an impressive menu of hearty dishes from chef Darren Jory to get stuck into. Rubbing shoulders with a number of farmers and suppliers around Exeter - the Rusty even reared its own pigs for a while - Darren seeks to showcase the seasons in his local menu.

Chef: **Darren Jory**. Lunch (Sunday only): **£10**. 3 course dinner from: **£30**. Seats: **100**

67 Howell Road, Exeter, Devon, EX4 4LZ.

T: 01392 214440

www.rustybike-exeter.co.uk

- The Rusty Bike
- @rustybikeexeter

79
The Galley Restaurant

A delightful and intimate dining spot in foodie Topsham, the Galley is a real find for lunch or dinner with your most favourite person.

Fish and seafood are the speciality, and the team prides itself on serving the very best produce – local seafood, Piper's Farm meat and fresh veggies – with waterside views of the River Exe. Vegetarians are well catered for too, and whatever you order, service is warm, friendly and efficient.

The set two or three course lunch is great value and recommended.

Chef: **Dolton Lodge**. 2 course set lunch from: **£17**. 3 course dinner from: **£32.50**. Seats: **48**

41 Fore Street, Topsham, Exeter, Devon, EX3 0HU.

T: 01392 876078

www.galleyrestaurant.co.uk

- The Galley Restaurant Topsham
- @galleytopsham

80
Rodean Restaurant

Over the last 16 years, chef Matthew Tilt and his wife Elizabeth have amassed a superb reputation and loyal following for their exciting, varied menus. Rodean lies in the stunning, unspoilt village of Kenton, just off the A379 and is a great setting for a relaxed and atmospheric dining experience. Ever changing seasonal menus, wine and dine evenings and special events add to the offering at this family restaurant with its focus on quality and consistency.

Chefs: **Matthew and Joshua Tilt**. 3 course lunch from: **£22**. 3 course dinner from: **£22**. Seats: **38**

The Triangle, Kenton, Exeter, Devon, EX6 8LS.
T: 01626 890195

www.rodeanrestaurant.co.uk
- Rodean Restaurant
- @rodean_kenton

82
The Horse

Take a wander round the historic Dartmoor town of Moretonhampstead before stopping off at The Horse, a great foodie find that provides wow factor dishes in a cool rustic setting. Its wood panelled bar area leads to the surprisingly light-filled Courtyard Restaurant where you can sample award winning food. Much of it, like the bread and bresaola, is made in-house, while an extensive pizza menu, Cornish scallops and Dartmoor venison that's prepared in the pub's own courtyard smokery, add gourmet delight.

Chef: **Christophe Ferraro**. 3 course lunch from: **£16**. 3 course dinner from: **£22**. Seats: **70**

7 George Street, Moretonhampstead, Devon, TQ13 8PG.
T: 01647 440242

www.thehorsedartmoor.co.uk
- The Horse (Moretonhampstead, UK)
- @horsedartmoor

81 ⓢ
The NoBody Inn

There's nothing quite like an authentic country pub, and the The NoBody Inn in Doddiscombsleigh is a great example of the genre. With oak beamed ceilings, an original 17th century bar and three cosy rooms above the inn (complete with four star AA rating), this dining destination has the quintessential rural pub experience down to a tee. Make sure to explore the noteworthy wine cellar alongside the equally impressive gourmet offering, and be warned, a whisky nightcap is inevitable when there are over 300 to choose from.

3 course lunch from: **£19**. 3 course dinner from: **£37**. Seats: **72**. Bedrooms: **5**. Room rate from: **£75**

Doddiscombsleigh, Exeter, Devon, EX6 7PS.
T: 01647 252394

www.nobodyinn.co.uk
- The Nobody Inn
- @thenobodyinn

83 ⓢ
Ilsington Country House Hotel and Spa

Set in ten acres of gardens and with views straight out over the rolling Dartmoor hills, this is a beautiful spot for a foodie break. Visit for a lazy lunch or a lingering evening meal in the two AA rosette restaurant with its seasonally inspired menus from chef Mike O'Donnell. There's also a more informal bistro for lighter meals. Little touches like home-smoked salmon and their own eggs add to the charm.

Chef: **Mike O'Donnell**. 3 course lunch from: **£22.50**. 3 course dinner from: **£38**. Seats: **50**. Bedrooms: **25**. Room rate from: **£125**

Ilsington, near Newton Abbot, Devon, TQ13 9RR.
T: 01364 661452

www.ilsington.co.uk
- Ilsington Country House Hotel
- @ilsingtonhotel

The Coach House by Michael Caines **No. 54**

84
The Cornish Arms

FABULOUS DINING PUB ON DARTMOOR

When John and Emma Hooker took over a refurbished coaching inn in the Dartmoor town of Tavistock three years ago, they set about creating the sort of pub they'd love to have as their local.

Their hospitality instincts paid off and the combination of hearty food done exceptionally well – chow down on ale battered fish and chips and

TRENCHERMAN'S AWARDS

BEST CHEF 2016

braised ox cheek with mash, horseradish cream and beef gravy, at very keen prices - are a winner. We like the plates of sharing nibbles and the smart outside courtyard for alfresco eating, too.

The pub has been included in the Top 50 Gastropubs 2016 and retained its Michelin Bib Gourmand, while head chef John took the top honours to be named Trencherman's Best Chef 2016.

Chef: **John Hooker**
3 course lunch from: **£23**
3 course dinner from: **£35**
Seats: **52**

15 West Street, Tavistock, Devon, PL19 8AN.
T: 01822 612145

www.thecornisharmstavistock.co.uk

Cornish Arms   @cornisharmstavy

85
Barbican Kitchen

The Tanner brothers' roomy, contemporary brasserie at the Plymouth Gin Distillery has just had a refurb to celebrate its 10th birthday. The décor is now as fresh as the daybout fish and Phillip Warren meat, and great use is made of cooking over charcoal on the Kamado Joe oven.

Chris and James Tanner have used their notable experience to create a variety of menus to keep everyone happy, including a pleasingly varied selection for vegetarians and vegans. Kids under five eat free.

Chefs: **Martyn Compton and David Boswell**.
3 course lunch from: **£12**. 3 course dinner from: **£28**. Seats: **100**

Plymouth Gin Distillery, 60 Southside Street, Plymouth, Devon, PL1 2LQ.
T: 01752 604448

www.barbicankitchen.com

Barbican Kitchen
@barbicankitchen

87
Boringdon Hall

A restaurant with atmosphere, on the edge of Dartmoor and surprisingly close to Plymouth, this 16th century manor house has a rich and romantic history. Enter the stunning Great Hall, past the stone fireplace and you'll be following in the footsteps of Elizabeth I. The restaurant overlooks the hall, and you can dine in comfort while hearing the gentle chatter of guests below and sound of logs crackling on the open fire. It's also open during the day for lunches and afternoon teas, and there's even a Boringdon Hall afternoon tea loyalty club.

Chef: **Chris Dyke**. 3 course lunch from: **£25**.
3 course dinner from: **£30**. Seats: **70**.
Bedrooms: **40**. Room rate from: **£109**

Colebrook, Plympton, Plymouth, Devon, PL7 4DP.
T: 01752 344455

www.boringdonhall.co.uk

Boringdon Hall Hotel
@boringdonhall
@boringdonhall

86
Langdon Court Restaurant

With head chef Jamie Rogers wiping the floor at the South West Chef of the Year Awards in 2015, guests can expect some exquisite food from the kitchen of this 16th century manor.

Set in acres of gorgeous gardens, Langdon Court is located just six miles from Plymouth, making it an ideal destination for lunch or dinner, as well as an indulgent midweek break. Whether you're visiting for high tea or the tasting menu, make sure to soak up a little of the hotel's history – Edward VII visited with Lily Langtry when he was Prince of Wales.

Chef: **Jamie Rogers**. 2 course lunch: **£12.95**, 3 course Sunday lunch: **£15.95**, 3 course dinner from: **£49.50**. Seats: **36**. Bedrooms: **18**. Room rate from: **£129**

Adam's Lane, Down Thomas, Plymouth, Devon, PL9 0DY.
T: 01752 862358

www.langdoncourt.com

Langdon Court Hotel & Restaurant
@langdoncourtuk

88
The Millbrook Inn

With it's distinctly pubby atmosphere, it's easy to see why The Millbrook is so popular. The team trawls local breweries for craft ales and carefully sources a great selection of wines. Food is in the safe hands of chef Jean-Philippe Bidart who keeps up the local sourcing theme, using Devon produce to create dishes with a touch of the French auberge. Great for families, there's space to run around, including a pretty courtyard and shallow stream for splashing about in.

You can even pop some coins in the honesty box and take home goods from its Veg Shed.

Chef: **Jean-Philippe Bidart**. 3 course lunch from: **£15**. Seats: **50**.

Southpool, Kingsbridge, Devon, TQ7 2RW.
T: 01548 531581

www.millbrookinnsouthpool.co.uk

Millbrook Inn
@southpoolducks

89
The Grill Room

Situated in what must be one of the most iconic buildings in Dartmouth, this appealing restaurant ticks all the right boxes for a great night out, whether you're after a romantic meal for two or a family gathering. The historic Royal Castle Hotel sits right on the inner harbour of this seaside town, a stately reminder of its nautical past. Stop for a drink in the buzzing traditional bar, then climb the stairs to the AA rosette restaurant, The Grill Room, where head chef Ankur Biswas uses the freshest seafood and select cuts of locally raised meat in delightful dishes.

Chef: **Ankur Biswas**. 3 course lunch from: **£19.50**. 3 course dinner from: **£27.50**. Seats: **60**. Bedrooms: **24**. Room rate from: **£160**

The Royal Castle Hotel, 11 The Quay, Dartmouth, Devon, TQ6 9PS.
T: 01803 833033

www.royalcastle.co.uk

The Royal Castle Hotel
@rchdartmouth1

90
Royal Seven Stars Hotel

A popular meeting place in the centre of Totnes since it opened as a traditional coaching inn in the 17th century, the Royal Seven Stars has broadened its horizons over the past four centuries with the addition of a stylish brasserie, sleek cocktail bar and comfortable rooms for weary travellers. Seek out the champagne bar for a crisp glass of fizz before heading next door to the TQ9 Brasserie for a sophisticated meal from head chef John Gallagher. Expect seasonal and local dishes such as Exmouth mussels, herb crusted lamb and Brixham's catch of the day.

Chef: **John Gallagher**. 3 course lunch from: **£22**. 3 course dinner from: **£27**. Seats: **35**. Bedrooms: **21**. Room rate from: **£125**

The Plains, Totnes, Devon, TQ9 5DD.
T: 01803 862125

www.royalsevenstars.co.uk

Royal Seven Stars Hotel
@rsstotnes

91
Dartington Hall

The impressive White Hart sits at the centre of Dartington Hall's stunning gardens and historic splendour. Its menu focuses on only the freshest, seasonal south Devon produce such as single suckled beef, grass reared lamb and local line caught fish. Expect dishes like curried mussels with leek, cumin, cream and coriander, and the famed Dartington beef burger with caramelised onion and Denhay mature cheddar. While you're there, make time to explore the 14th century hall - it's well worth it.

Chef: **Anuj Thakur**. 3 course lunch from: **£21**. 3 course dinner from: **£25**. Seats: **38**. Bedrooms: **50**. Room rate from: **£49.50pp**

Dartington, Totnes, Devon, TQ9 6EL.
T: 01803 847150

www.dartingtonhall.com

Dartington Hall
@dartingtonhall

92
The Orange Tree Restaurant

Just a few steps away from the harbour in Torquay, this highly popular restaurant is famed for its modern British and European cuisine and exceptional hospitality. Inspired by abundant and exceptional local produce, Bernd and his wife Sharon are passionate about showcasing only the finest West Country ingredients. Shellfish and fish from Brixham market, beef and free range duck direct from their local farm are just a couple of highlights on a regularly refreshed menu. New for this year is a stunning tasting menu that enables guests to sample a little of everything.

Chef: **Bernd Wolf**. 3 course dinner from: **£28**. Seats: **42**

14-16 Parkhill Road, Torquay, Devon, TQ1 2AL.
T: 01803 213936

www.orangetreerestaurant.co.uk

The Orange Tree Restaurant
@orangetreerest
@orangetreetorquay

Barbican Kitchen **No. 85**

CORNWALL

The Idle Rocks **No. 110**

93. Langmans Restaurant
94. Talland Bay Hotel
95. Q Restaurant at the Old Quay House Hotel
96. Asquiths Restaurant
97. The Carlyon Bay Hotel
98. Restaurant Nathan Outlaw
99. Outlaw's Fish Kitchen
100. The Seafood Restaurant
101. St Petroc's Bistro
102. Rick Stein's Cafe
103. The Cornish Arms
104. The Green Room
105. Jamie Oliver's Fifteen Cornwall
106. Zacry's at Watergate Bay Hotel
107. Saffron
108. Tabb's Restaurant
109. The Quarterdeck at The Nare
110. The Idle Rocks
111. The Water's Edge
112. Pendennis Restaurant at The Royal Duchy Hotel
113. Mullion Cove Hotel
114. Rick Stein, Porthleven
115. Kota
116. Roswarne Manor Restaurant
117. Halsetown Inn
118. Porthminster Beach Cafe
119. The Victoria Inn
120. Ben's Cornish Kitchen
121. The Bay at Hotel Penzance
122. Harris's Restaurant
123. The Springer Spaniel
124. The Wellington Hotel
125. St Moritz Hotel
126. The Mariners Public House
127. Trevalsa Court Hotel and Restaurant
128. Fistral Beach Hotel and Spa
129. Quies Restaurant at Treglos Hotel
130. Rose in Vale Country House Hotel
131. The Watch House
132. Oliver's
133. Samphire Bistro
134. Rick Stein's Fish
135. The Ferryboat Inn
136. The Bay Hotel
137. Alba
138. Tolcarne Inn
139. 2 Fore Street Restaurant

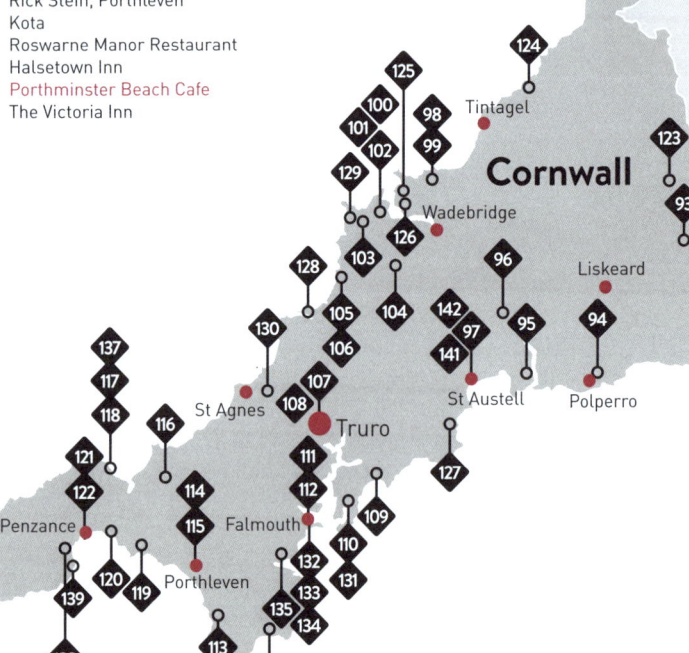

Restaurants listed in the guide correspond to the numbers plotted on the map. Locations are approximate.

New restaurants to the guide are highlighted in red.

93
Langmans Restaurant

A SPECIAL EXPERIENCE IN CALLINGTON

Langmans has been wowing diners for over 15 years and chef Anton Buttery's passion for the art of cookery stands out a mile.

Anton is a stickler for detail, and the award winning chef personally seeks out seasonal ingredients from his hand picked suppliers - from beef farmers to cheese dairies, only the finest will do.

Langmans's tasting menus are beautifully constructed with delicate flavours that contrast and excite. And with Anton's wife Gail running front of house, you'll also receive the warmest of welcomes.

Chef: **Anton Buttery**
7 course evening tasting menu: **£45**
Seats: **24**

3 Church Street, Callington, Cornwall, PL17 7RE.
T: 01579 384933

www.langmansrestaurant.co.uk

 Langmans Restaurant
 @langmansdining

94
Talland Bay Hotel

ART AND FOOD COMBINE IN A COASTAL COVE SETTING

There are plenty of romantic legends associated with Talland Bay, the blissfully beautiful cove once frequented by smugglers.

And arriving at the hotel that's set above Talland's two beaches feels like discovering a hidden treasure, especially with the beautiful award winning gardens framing the view out to sea, and the multitude of quirky artworks – inside and out.

Another find comes in the form of two AA rosette cooking from long standing chef Nick Hawke. His imaginative and appealing dishes are best enjoyed over a long, lingering dinner, but you can also pop in for a brasserie style lunch, perhaps while exploring the South West Coast Path which runs right past the hotel.

Chef: **Nick Hawke**
3 course lunch from: **£25**
3 course dinner from: **£42**
Seats: **40**
Bedrooms: **23**
Room rate from: **£125**

Porthallow, Looe, Cornwall, PL13 2JB.
T: 01503 272667

www.tallandbayhotel.co.uk

 Talland Bay Hotel
 @tallandbayhotel
 @tallandbay

95

Q Restaurant at the Old Quay House Hotel

STYLISH DINING AT THE WATER'S EDGE

This smart boutique hotel is a little gem hidden in plain sight in the middle of Fowey's busy Fore Street. Go through the stylish champagne bar and elegant restaurant at the back of the building and stunning views of the estuary open before you. There's even a small terrace where you can dine, which, in the setting sun with a glass of good fizz in your hand, is a rather fabulous experience.

Chef Ryan Kellow's menus are modern European in style and well executed, and after a great meal, it's a pleasure to head upstairs to the newly refurbished bedrooms.

Chef: **Ryan Kellow**
3 course lunch from: **£25**
3 course dinner from: **£37.50**
Seats: **36**
Bedrooms: **11**
Room rate from: **£145**

28 Fore Street, Fowey, Cornwall, PL23 1AQ.
T: 01726 833302

www.theoldquayhouse.com

- The Old Quay House Hotel
- @theoldquayhouse
- @oldquayhouse

96

Asquiths Restaurant

DINING PERFECTION IN DELIGHTFUL LOSTWITHIEL

As a result of the Eden Project, Lostwithiel has become increasingly chic in recent years and is now one of Cornwall's hubs for antiques and homewares. Of course, shopping is hungry work and the very best way of rewarding yourself must be a visit to the delightful Asquiths for dinner.

Chef patron Graham Cuthbertson's modern British cooking displays the chef's experience and confidence, with a pleasingly restrained number of dishes on the menu – all the better to showcase local produce in dishes such as gurnard fillet with potato puree, brown shrimp beurre blanc, charred broccoli and capers. Front of house service led by Graham's wife Sally ensures you are well looked after.

Chef: **Graham Cuthbertson**
3 course dinner from: **£28**
Seats: **28**

19 North Street, Lostwithiel, Cornwall, PL22 0EF.
T: 01208 871714

www.asquithsrestaurant.co.uk

- Asquiths Restaurant
- @asquiths_dining

97
The Carlyon Bay Hotel

GLAMOROUS DINING OVERLOOKING THE BAY

Gleaming silver, deco-style mirrors and smart white leather furniture makes the recently refurbished main restaurant at The Carlyon Bay Hotel a very glamorous experience – only heightened by the large picture windows that look over an expansive seascape.

Head chef Paul Leakey has been with the hotel for many years and his experience shows in fine dining dishes in the restaurant and modern cooking in the adjacent Taste Brasserie. He's a huge fan of Asian cuisine, and you'll find the influence in a number of dishes. In addition to lunch and dinner, the spa, golf course and entertainments make this a great spot for a classic British gourmet getaway.

Chef: **Paul Leakey**
3 course lunch from: **£18.50**
3 course dinner from: **£38**
Seats: **220**
Bedrooms: **86**
Room rate from: **£75**

Sea Road, St Austell, Cornwall, PL25 3RD.
T: 01726 812304

www.carlyonbay.com

- The Carlyon Bay Hotel
- @carlyonbayhotel

98
Restaurant Nathan Outlaw

NEW SETTING FOR MICHELIN CHEF

With its move to a new location with stunning sea views at Port Isaac, Restaurant Nathan Outlaw is flying high. Two Michelin stars, four AA rosettes and a lofty fourth position in the *Good Food Guide 2016* tells you all you need to know.

Nathan's championing Cornish seafood as ever, in fact, it's all that's on the lunchtime or evening set menus, and the cooking is fresh, innovative and beautiful. There's great pleasure to be had in putting yourself in the hands of this culinary Neptune and letting him wow you with his powers. There's a full menu choice whether you eat downstairs or upstairs, although it's a little more relaxed down in the kitchen bar.

Chefs: **Nathan Outlaw and Chris Simpson**
4 course lunch: **£59**
Dinner tasting menu: **£119**
Seats: **30**

6 New Road, Port Isaac, Cornwall, PL29 3SB.
T: 01208 880896

www.nathan-outlaw.com

- @resnathanoutlaw
- @nathanoutlaw

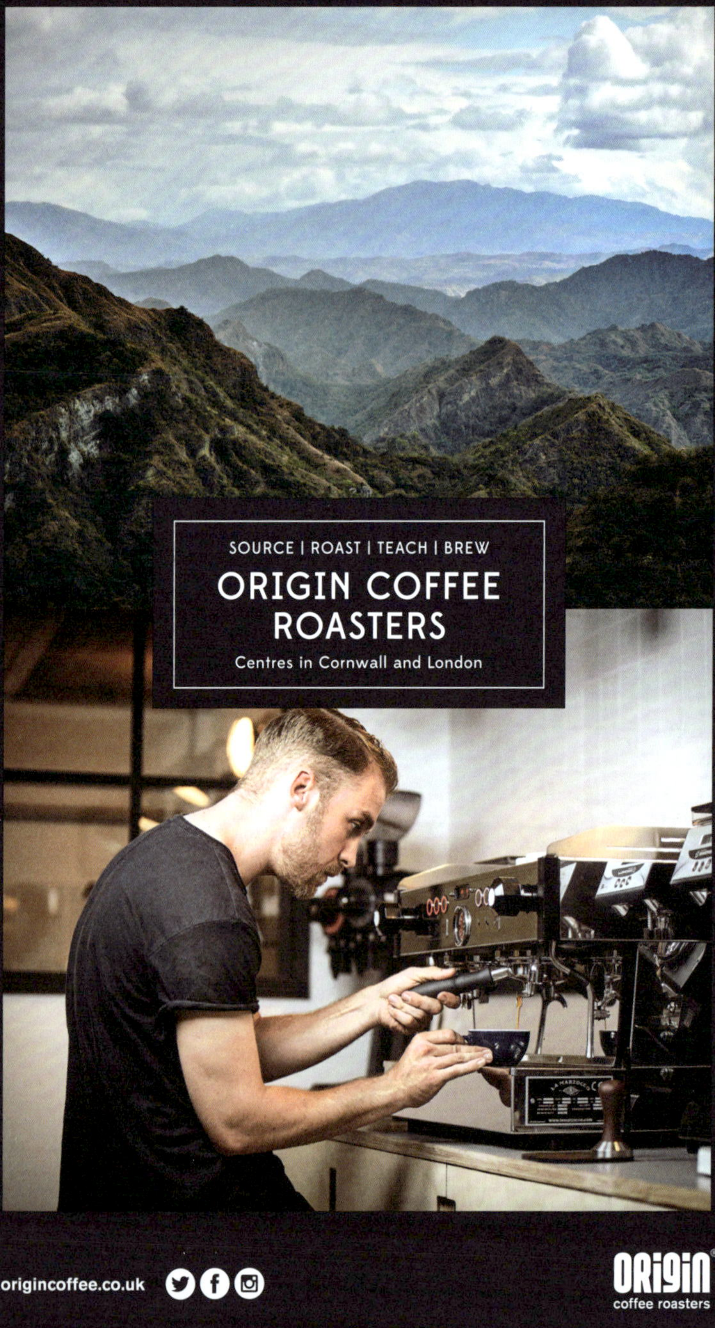
SOURCE | ROAST | TEACH | BREW
ORIGIN COFFEE ROASTERS
Centres in Cornwall and London
origincoffee.co.uk
ORIGIN
coffee roasters

99
Outlaw's Fish Kitchen

FAMED FOOD IN A FISHERMAN'S COTTAGE

This tiny but hugely atmospheric 15th century fisherman's cottage overlooking the harbour in Port Isaac is another appealing way to enjoy the Nathan Outlaw experience. This time it's a little more relaxed, and in a very Mediterranean way the menu is created from the freshest seafood that's been landed from the surrounding waters each day.

The catch is turned into small plates of delicious morsels, so you can choose as many or few as you like.

Chef: **Tim Barnes**
Lunch plates from: **£6-£20**
Dinner plates from: **£6-£20**
Seats: **24**

1 Middle Street, Port Isaac, Cornwall, PL29 3RH.
T: 01208 881183

www.outlaws.co.uk/fishkitchen

- @fish_kitchen
- @fishkitchen

100
The Seafood Restaurant

PURE PISCATORIAL CLASS

It's the restaurant that Rick Stein and Padstow are most famous for, and the bedrock of Rick and Jill's collection of polished piscatorial places.

Smart, contemporary European in style, you can expect seriously good food served with sophistication and fine wines.

Head chef Stephane Delourme has made this place his own over many years, delivering classy cooking inspired by the local catch, Cornish produce, his Breton background and Rick's gastronomic travels. The result is a pan-global menu that's adroitly done.

Start the evening with drinks at the seductive bar and finish (in good weather) with coffee on the outdoor terrace.

Chef: **Stephane Delourme**
3 course lunch from: **£31**
3 course dinner from: **£40.90**
Seats: **130**
Bedrooms: **16 (and an additional 6 in St Edmund's House)**
Room rate from: **£154**

Riverside, Padstow, Cornwall, PL28 8BY.
T: 01841 532700

www.rickstein.com

- Rick and Jill Stein - The Seafood
- @theseafood
- @theseafood

101
St Petroc's Bistro

CLASSIC BISTRO FOOD IN ELEGANT BACKSTREET SETTING

A couple of minutes' stroll from the harbour, and up a quiet backstreet is one of Padstow's hidden havens. With its neat box hedging and covered porch, St Petroc's is an elegant building (the fifth oldest in Padstow) and a perfect retreat from the often bustling seaside town.

One of the Stein family of restaurants, it serves classic bistro style dishes, with a flavour of the Med and a great choice of fish dishes, along with a superb selection of well-aged steaks. There's a cosy combination of rooms containing rustic wooden tables and chairs, leather sofas and patio doors on to a pretty courtyard. Upstairs bedrooms are similarly individual and comfy.

Chef: **Nick Evans**
3 course lunch from: **£20**
3 course dinner from: **£28.65**
Seats: **50**
Bedrooms: **10 (and an additional 4 in Prospect House)**
Room rate from: **£160**

4 New Street, Padstow, Cornwall, PL28 8EA.
T: 01841 532700

www.rickstein.com

- St Petroc's Bistro
- @theseafood
- @theseafood

102
Rick Stein's Cafe

FOR CHILLED GLOBAL GOURMETS

Get a taste of the Stein experience with a lighter price tag at the Stein's charming, beachy cafe. Weatherboard walls, vibrant colours and lots of wood says modern Cornwall, while the menu cherry picks from across the globe.

South east Asian, north African, Indian and Mediterranean cuisines are sifted for inspiration such as a whole deep fried seabass with chilli sauce on the dinner menu, and Mounts Bay sardines with sea salt and lime for lunch.

With plenty of meat and veggie dishes, a children's' menu, exotic breakfasts plus coffee and pastries, it's an all-day crowd-pleaser.

Chef: **Mark O'Hagan**
3 course lunch from: **£23.50**
3 course dinner from: **£28.72**
Seats: **36**
Bedrooms: **3**
Room rate from: **£113**

Middle Street, Padstow, Cornwall, PL28 8AP.
T: 01841 532700

www.rickstein.com

- Rick Stein's Cafe
- @theseafood
- @theseafood

103
The Cornish Arms

STEIN'S CLASSIC CORNISH PUB

For classic pub food created with a hefty dose of flair in a rustic country setting, plan a stop off at The Cornish Arms in St Merryn.

With easy-to-choose-from menus based on Rick Stein's recipes, there's plenty of choice – from Sunday roasts to world curries to steaming bowls of fresh, local mussels.

The pub has been simply but beautifully restored and decorated by Jill Stein to create a large, airy dining room which is very family friendly and a cosy traditional bar in which to find a corner and enjoy a pint. There's also a large outdoor eating area, making this a great supper spot with sandy kids after a day on the beach.

Chef: **Alex Clark**
3 course lunch from: **£20.85**
3 course dinner from: **£20.85**
Seats: **100**

Churchtown, St Merryn, Cornwall,
PL28 8ND.
T: 01841 532700

www.rickstein.com

- Cornish Arms
- @thecornisharms
- @theseafood

104
The Green Room

SMART SURFY RESTAURANT WITH FIELD TO FORK DELIGHTS

As the name suggests, it's all about the Cornish surf scene at The Green Room at Retallack Resort and Spa on the north Cornwall coast. Not that you need to be a salty haired surf dude to enjoy the quality cooking because this is a smart restaurant with contemporary cuisine that just happens to have surf boards suspended from the ceiling and a FlowRider artificial wave next door.

Specialising in the finest food Cornwall has to offer and delights like edible flowers, foraged finds and local seafood from Newlyn - it's a find for a romantic dinner, supper with chums or lunch with the kids.

3 course lunch from: **£15**
3 course dinner from: **£30**
Seats: **80**
Bedrooms: **23**
Room rate from: **£79**

Retallack Resort and Spa,
Winnards Perch, St Columb Major,
Cornwall, TR9 6DE.
T: 01637 882480

www.retallackresort.co.uk

- The Green Room Restaurant
- @greenroom_rr
- @green_room_restaurant

105
Jamie Oliver's Fifteen Cornwall

ITALIAN INSPIRED, FEEL-GOOD FOOD

With its wall of windows overlooking Watergate Bay, Fifteen Cornwall is a spectacular spot for breakfast, lunch or dinner, as you watch surfers compete for a wave, or the sun go down over the Cornish seascape.

The restaurant is a social enterprise that trains local young people to become professional chefs through its award winning Apprentice Programme. The chefs create Italian inspired, rustic food using carefully sourced ingredients.

With its contemporary styling, buzzy vibe, friendly service, jaw dropping location and assured, honest cooking, this is a modern Cornwall must-visit. And the "all profits go to the Apprentice Programme" element makes the experience even sweeter.

3 course lunch from: **£32**
3 course dinner from: **£42**
5 course tasting menu: **£65**
Seats: **120**

On the beach, Watergate Bay, Cornwall, TR8 4AA.
T: 01637 861000

www.fifteencornwall.co.uk

- Fifteen Cornwall
- @fifteencornwall
- @fifteencornwall

106 $ ▢
Zacry's at Watergate Bay Hotel

BUZZY NEW YORK-STYLE BRASSERIE OVERLOOKING THE BAY

Zacry's brings a slice of the Big Apple to Cornwall, with its American-inspired contemporary brasserie style. Chevron flooring, zinc topped tables and large picture windows make this a great spot for relaxed daytime feasting on the likes of deep fried rabbit and slaw or grilled lobster.

However, as the sun sets and the vintage style filament bulbs dim, the buzzy clatter of the open kitchen makes you move a little closer for conversation, and turns this into a much more intimate dining experience. Executive chef Neil Haydock uses fresh Cornish produce in the creative and crowd-pleasing menus that are big on meat and seafood dishes cooked in the indoor charcoal oven.

Chef: **Neil Haydock**
2 course evening menu from: **£29.50**
3 course evening menu from: **£36.50**
Seats: **120**
Bedrooms: **69**
Room rate from: **£160**

On The Beach, Watergate Bay, Cornwall, TR8 4AA.
T: 01637 861231

www.zacrys.com

- Watergate Bay Hotel
- @watergatebay
- @watergatebay

107
Saffron

DINKY AND DELIGHTFUL IN TRURO

This stylish, intimate restaurant should be on the hit list for any dining excursion in Truro, as head chef Nik Tinney has delighted diners here for over 10 years.

The restaurant has been completely renovated in recent times, to create an interior which equally matches the standard of food. It's stylish, especially the snazzy bar which is a great place to sit and enjoy a pre dinner drink. Old features have been retained and simple wooden tables and flagstone floors, along with cosy candlelit booths and a wood burner create a timeless, Cornish feel.

Nik is a champion for Cornish produce, which features strongly on his menus so you'll often find him sourcing ingredients at local markets.

Chef: **Nik Tinney**
3 course lunch from: **£18**
3 course dinner from: **£25**
Seats: **45**

5 Quay Street, Truro, Cornwall, TR1 2HB.
T: 0872 263771

www.saffronrestauranttruro.co.uk

- Saffron Truro
- @tsaffrontruro
- @saffrontruro

TRENCHERMAN'S COLLECTIONS

Take five for seafood by the sea

46 HIX Oyster and Fish House
Stunning views across the Jurassic coast are the backdrop for spankingly fresh seafood from Mark Hix's Lyme Regis team.

98 Restaurant Nathan Outlaw
Nathan's new location at Port Isaac provides a stunning spot for his two Michelin-starred seafood tasting menus.

118 Porthminster Beach Cafe
Slip on your flip flops and trundle up the beach for crispy fried squid and monkfish curry with lots of Asian influence at the St Ives beach cafe.

100 The Seafood Restaurant
Head chef Stephane Delourme's assured cooking at this Padstow institution makes it a perennial favourite.

50 WestBeach
It doesn't get much more authentic than eating fresh seafood by the sea in Bournemouth - landed by the restaurant's own dayboats.

108
Tabb's Restaurant

TRURO'S LITTLE GEM

There's a lot of restaurants making a lot of noise in Cornwall's ever expanding dining scene, but this is one Cornish gem that doesn't need to shout to shine.

Tucked away in a quiet side street, Tabb's Restaurant has been feeding Truro's fine dining foodies for the past 10 years, gaining a loyal following along the way.

Housed in a former pub, bar stools and tankards have been traded in for uncluttered design, putting emphasis on chef patron Nigel Tabb's impressive kitchen craft. Everything you eat here is made by the man himself, from the freshly baked bread to the handmade chocolates, and sourced from his close knit network of Cornish suppliers.

Chef: **Nigel Tabb**
3 course lunch from: **£25**
3 course dinner from: **£25**
Seats: **28**

85 Kenwyn Street, Truro, Cornwall, TR1 3BZ.
T: 01872 262110

www.tabbs.co.uk

Tabb's Restaurant
@nigeltabb

109
The Quarterdeck at The Nare

FOOD TO MATCH THE VIEWS AT CLASSIC HOTEL

With its yachty décor, classic European dishes and sunny terrace overlooking a beautiful Cornish beach, a visit to The Quarterdeck at The Nare is a little like taking a trip back in time to the very best kind of classic British hotel. No surprise then to discover that it's been in the Ashworth family for many years.

The food is every bit as good as the views and created with skill and precision by chef Richard James using the freshly caught and abundant seafood, as well as treats such as locally reared beef.

If you can stay the night, the large heated outdoor pool and flower filled cocktail terrace will also delight.

Chef: **Richard James**
3 course lunch from: **£23**
3 course dinner from: **£40**
Seats: **60, 100 in the summer on the terrace**
Bedrooms: **37**
Room rate from: **£290**

Carne Beach, Veryan-in-Roseland, Truro, Cornwall, TR2 5PF.
T: 01872 500000

www.quarterdeckrestaurant.co.uk

The Nare Hotel
@thenarehotel

110
The Idle Rocks

BOUTIQUE CHIC AND EXQUISITE HARBOUR VIEWS

Chic and contemporary, this boutique hotel and restaurant is the epitome of the modern Cornish vibe, all tutti frutti mid tones, white light, sea views and sumptuous dining.

Perched right on the harbourside of St Mawes, the long frontage offers exquisite sea views and dining opportunities on the terrace. This is a place to re-engage with life's simple pleasures: break homemade bread and sip good wine as the sun sets, before getting stuck in to a vibrant menu crafted from local ingredients, courtesy of new head chef Guy Owen.

Chef: **Guy Owen**
3 course lunch from: **£35**
3 course dinner from: **£45**
Seats: **65**
Bedrooms: 19
Room rate from: **£200**

Harbourside, St Mawes, Cornwall, TR2 5AN.
T: 01326 270270

www.idlerocks.com

- The Idle Rocks
- @theidlerocks
- @idlerocks

111
The Water's Edge

FABULOUS SEAFOOD ON FALMOUTH'S HISTORIC HARBOUR

There's a reason The Greenbank Hotel called its two AA rosette restaurant The Water's Edge; with panoramic views across Falmouth harbour and out to the estuary, guests enjoy a privileged perspective on the dayboats bobbing about in the water below.

With a vista like this it's only right that head chef Nick Hodges and his brigade of chefs use the freshest seafood to craft a menu littered with the Cornish catch. Local meat and vegetarian dishes are also included on the comprehensive menu of course, and there's a carefully put together wine list to imbibe as you drink in the views.

Chef: **Nick Hodges**
3 course lunch from: **£20**
3 course dinner from: **£35**
Seats: **70**
Bedrooms: **60**
Room rate from: **£99**

The Greenbank Hotel, Harbourside, Falmouth, Cornwall, TR11 2SR.
T: 01326 312440

www.greenbank-hotel.co.uk

- The Greenbank Hotel
- @greenbankhotel
- @greenbankhotel

Make yours a Frobishers.

Treat your taste buds to a flavour adventure with Frobishers Juices, lovingly crafted from fruits picked, pressed and squeezed at their prime to capture all those vibrant colours and natural flavours. We never compromise on taste, so why should you?

Find Frobishers juices, still and sparkling juice drinks and smoothies lining the fridges of many of your favourite pubs, bars and restaurants across the UK.

E. SALES@FROBISHERS.COM | T. 01392 825333 | WWW.FROBISHERS.COM | FOLLOW US @FROBISHERS

112
Pendennis Restaurant at The Royal Duchy Hotel

CLASSIC BRITISH COOKING WITH FABULOUS VIEWS

Elegant dining is the order of the day at Pendennis Restaurant – you might even get a little live piano accompaniment to your dining experience.

Do drinks on the leafy terrace to start – the views are fabulous – before moving in to the recently refurbished restaurant for high quality dining that makes good use of the local catch.

A classic British hotel with arguably the best views in Falmouth, this is a refined getaway with great comfort and facilities.

Chef: **John Mijatovic**
3 course lunch from: **£20**
3 course dinner from: **£39**
Seats: **100**
Bedrooms:**45**
Room rate from: **£70**

Cliff Road, Falmouth, Cornwall, TR11 4NX.
T: 01326 313042

www.royalduchy.com

The Royal Duchy Hotel
@brendhotels

113
Mullion Cove Hotel

VICTORIAN HOTEL WITH CONTEMPORARY COOKING

This grand Victorian hotel - a legacy of the great railway age - sits high on the cliffs in a dramatic spot on the Lizard Peninsula.

It truly merits the "unrivalled views" label with a panorama that encompasses a broad sweep of ocean and dramatic wave-battered cliffs and the old fishing harbour in the cove below.

A slice of modern sophistication comes in the form of chef Paul Stephens. Returning to his Cornish roots after working in high profile establishments such as The Dorchester, The Ritz and the Fat Duck, he's continuing the hotel's legacy of producing excellent food that draws people to its two AA rosette restaurant.

Chef: **Paul Stephens**
3 course lunch from: **£18**
3 course dinner from: **£35**
Seats: **60**
Bedrooms:**30**
Room rate from: **£95**

Mullion Cove, Helston, Cornwall, TR12 7EP.
T: 01326 240328

www.mullion-cove.co.uk

Mullion Cove Hotel
@mullioncove

114
Rick Stein, Porthleven

SOPHISTICATED COOL BY THE HARBOUR

Jill Stein's fabulous seasidey decor at this harbourside restaurant is the epitome of modern Cornish cool. Whitewashed walls, sea bright metal chairs and lots of bare wood creates a contemporary and relaxing vibe.

Sharing platters of globally-inspired dishes – with plenty of seafood, naturally - are delightful to fight over with your main squeeze, but work well as a main for one too. Then move on to the pick of the day's catch that's simply prepared, or dishes such as Singapore chilli crab and rib eye steak.

A pleasingly restrained but sophisticated cocktail and wine list accompanies, and makes this a good spot for an aperitif on the first floor terrace, and a destination for lunch or dinner.

Chef: **Simon Allott**
3 course lunch from: **£21.50**
3 course dinner from: **£30.24**
Seats: **75**

Mount Pleasant, Porthleven, Cornwall, TR13 9JS.
T: 01326 565636

www.rickstein.com

- Rick Stein, Porthleven
- @steinporthleven
- @theseafood

115
Kota

ASIAN-INSPIRED FINE DINING

One of only a handful of Cornish restaurants to hold a Michelin Bib Gourmand, a visit to this harbourside restaurant with its rustic and atmospheric interior, is a huge delight.

Kota's head chef, the half Maori, half Chinese Malay Jude Kereama (who represented the South West in BBC Two's *Great British Menu*), creates beautiful, Asian-inspired menus using local produce. Over the years, Jude and his wife Jane have built a loyal following for Kota's award winning food, extensive wine list and relaxed, attentive service.

The restaurant also has two B&B rooms – one with great harbour views – making it an even more attractive proposition.

Chef: **Jude Kereama**
3 course dinner from: **£21**
Seats: **32**
Bedrooms: **2**
Room rate from: **£70**

Harbour Head, Porthleven, Cornwall, TR13 9JA.
T: 01326 562407

www.kotarestaurant.co.uk

- Kota
- @kota_kai

St Moritz Hotel **No. 125**

SINCE 1989

HILDON
NATURAL MINERAL WATER

AN ENGLISH NATURAL MINERAL WATER OF EXCEPTIONAL TASTE
FROM THE HILDON ESTATE IN THE TEST VALLEY, HAMPSHIRE.

Hildon Ltd, Broughton, Hampshire, SO20 8DQ
www.hildon.com +44 (0) 1794 301 747

116

Rosewarne Manor Restaurant

FINE DINING IN THE CORNISH COUNTRYSIDE

Hidden away in lush countryside near Hayle, this is a great gourmet stop when travelling through Cornwall as well as a fine dining destination. Choose from head chef Phil Thomas' informal bar menu, go grill-style with a prime steak, or delight in the high quality, modern British à la carte.

Definitely worth checking out is the tasting menu which takes place on the last Friday of each month and showcases local ingredients crafted into fine dining dishes.

Relaxed and informal, the outside terrace is also a lovely spot for supper on a summer's evening.

Chef: **Phil Thomas**
3 course lunch from: **£20**
3 course dinner from: **£32**
Seats: **36, and function room and private dining**

20 Gwinear Road, Connor Downs, Hayle, Cornwall, TR27 5JQ.
T: 01209 610414

www.rosewarnemanor.co.uk

 Rosewarne Manor Restaurant & function venue
 @rosewarnemanor

117

Halsetown Inn

ASIA MEETS THE MED IN CORNWALL

Now in its fourth year, the Halsetown team has well and truly secured the pub's foodie credentials, becoming a destination venue for relaxed, pan-global dining.

Part of its appeal, along with the granite walls, flagstone floors and open fires, is due to chef Ange Baxter's unique menus. She fuses Asian and Mediterranean flavours with aplomb to create a quirky take on pub classics.

The whole team is passionate about the inn's ethical and sustainable credentials, which of course means local producers are at the heart of the operation. Its Michelin Bib Gourmand is well deserved.

Chef: **Ange Baxter**
3 course lunch from: **£16**
3 course dinner from: **£20**
Seats: **80**

Halsetown, St Ives, Cornwall, TR26 3NA.
T: 01736 795583

www.halsetowninn.co.uk

 Halsetown Inn
 @halsetowninn
 @halsetowninn

118
Porthminster Beach Cafe

GET FRESH AT THE BEACH

This multi award-winning restaurant sits right on the beach at St Ives.

The stunning quality of light that surrounds this far point of Cornwall is reflected in the breezy, clean white interior of the restaurant, and with its large outside terrace it has a distinctly Mediterranean feel - despite the Asian inspired seafood menu.

Created out of a strip of waste ground, there's also a veg, herb and salad garden which provides plentiful amounts of produce for chef Ryan Venning's busy kitchen.

Open daily from breakfast through to the evening, Porthminster has wide appeal and dining at night, looking out at the moonlit ocean is a real treat.

Chef: **Ryan Venning**
3 course lunch from: **£25**
3 course dinner from: **£40**
Seats: **82**

Porthminster Beach, St Ives, Cornwall, TR26 2EB.
T: 01736 795352

www.porthminstercafe.co.uk
- Porthminster Cafe
- @porthbcafe
- @porthminstercafe

119
The Victoria Inn

IMPRESSIVE PUB DINING

Since taking over one of Cornwall's oldest pubs in 2014, Nik and Laura Boyle have done well to retain The Victoria's traditional charm while making their mark and adding contemporary touches.

First there's the award winning food from Nik and his team, which cleverly blends classic Cornish produce with 21st century creativity. Then there are the new lodgings above the inn, offering a comfortable and stylish stay for those travelling through the quaint village of Perranuthnoe. Popular with locals and visitors alike, one thing the couple promise they'll be keeping their hands off, however, is the pub's iconic pink exterior.

Chef: **Nik Boyle**
3 course lunch from: **£25**
3 course dinner from: **£25**
Seats: **60**
Bedrooms: **2**
Room rate from: **£75**

Perranuthnoe, Penzance, Cornwall, TR20 9NP.
T: 01736 710309

www.victoriainn-penzance.co.uk
- Victoria Inn Perranuthnoe
- @victoriaperran
- @therealvictoriainn

120
Ben's Cornish Kitchen

CRACKING COOKING AT A NEW CORNISH CLASSIC

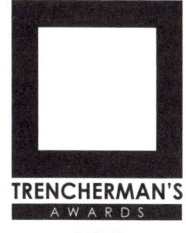

TRENCHERMAN'S AWARDS
BEST RESTAURANT 2016

This is a dining must-visit in Cornwall, and since its cracking Jay Rayner review is almost as much of a local landmark as the famous St Michael's Mount itself.

The bistro style, family-run restaurant in the heart of Marazion is just a few steps from the famous castle causeway and led by chef patron Ben Prior, with brother Toby on sous chef duties and mum Jayne and friend Rob running front of house.

Ben throws all his culinary passion and love of great food and wine into his Cornish Kitchen and consequently the excellently priced set menus are a treat, always offering something new to the steady stream of visitors who travel across the county to eat here. It goes without saying that local and seasonal ingredients are at the core of the offering and you'll find an excellent, hand-picked selection of wines to accompany the delightful dishes.

Chef: **Ben Prior**
3 course set lunch: **£20**
3 course dinner from: **£29**
Seats: **35**

Marazion, Penzance, Cornwall, TR17 0EL.
T: 01736 719200

www.benscornishkitchen.com

 Ben's Cornish Kitchen    @cornishkitchen

HAVE YOU GOT THE
APPETITE
for Adventure?

Join Michelin star chef Nathan Outlaw & Sharp's Brewery on the Beer & Food Adventure, where you'll discover the source of his quality ingredients and visit our home, Sharp's Brewery, for a tour and master class in beer tasting. All this before sitting down to dinner, prepared by Nathan, in a secret, remote Cornish location making your dining experience truly incredible.

THERE'S AN ADVENTURE BREWING

  #SHARPSADVENTURE

ENTER AT **SHARPSADVENTURE.CO.UK**

121
The Bay at Hotel Penzance

LOVELY CORNISH DINING WITH COASTAL VIEWS

A plate of fresh seafood and a glass of something great while watching the waves lap at the shore is a must at The Bay in Penzance.

Holding down two AA rosettes for nine years is no mean feat, but head chef Ben Reeve's winning combination of great Cornish ingredients and inspired world flavours, with a little help from the local fishermen's hauls, certainly warrants its success.

Twenty five modern rooms and nothing's-too-much-trouble service make this a comfortable spot. On sunny days the terrace of this Victorian hotel could easily be mistaken for the Mediterranean, so eat alfresco if you can.

Chef: **Ben Reeve**
3 course lunch from: **£20**
3 course dinner from: **£32**
Seats: **40**
Bedrooms: **25**
Room rate from: **£80**

Britons Hill, Penzance, Cornwall, TR18 3AE.
T: 01736 366890

www.thebaypenzance.co.uk

The Bay Restaurant
@perfectpenzance

122
Harris's Restaurant

CLASSIC DINING IN PENZANCE

Of all the restaurants in Penzance, none have the well-loved longevity of Harris's, which has been run by the same family for 30 years.

Small but perfectly formed, Harris's has won loyal fans for its beautifully prepared and freshly cooked seafood which is landed at nearby Newlyn. Meat lovers are also well catered for with quality beef and lamb sourced from Cornish farms. In addition, chef Roger Harris is famed for his desserts such as iced lemon soufflé in a dark chocolate case.

The wine list is extensive and the service suitably attentive too.

Chef: **Roger Harris**
3 course lunch from: **£27.50**
3 course dinner from: **£27.50**
Seats: **20 in the restaurant, 20 in the bar**

46 New Street, Penzance, Cornwall, TR18 2LZ.
T: 01736 364408

www.harrissrestaurant.co.uk

CORNWALL

123
The Springer Spaniel

The kitchen at this sister dining pub to Anton Piotrowski's Treby Arms is led by head chef Alistair Fraser. So, as you'd expect with this pedigree, food is the big attraction at the modern country inn. Choose from pub classics, treat yourself to à la carte dining, or unleash your inner gourmet and go for the tasting menu with matched wine flight. It's guaranteed to get tails wagging.

Chef: **Alistair Fraser**.
Lunch courses from: **£8.50**. 3 course dinner from: **£35**. Seats: **42**

Treburley, Launceston, Cornwall, PL15 9NS.
T: 01579 370424

www.thespringerspaniel.co.uk

- The Springer Spaniel
- @springerthe

124 ⓢ
The Wellington Hotel

Nestled in the cliffs overlooking Boscastle Harbour, The Wellington Hotel enjoys an enviable position on the north Cornwall coast. Housed in one of the county's oldest coaching inns, head chef Kit Davis' food both honours the restaurant's public house tradition and draws on contemporary European dining, so expect classics like Cornish cider mussels alongside more refined options such as the roasted beef rump with chorizo and olives. Bring the kids and four-legged friends along too, as everyone is welcome at this relaxed dining spot.

Chef: **Kit Davis**. 3 course lunch from: **£25**.
3 course dinner from: **£37.50**. Seats: **25**.
Bedrooms: **17**. Room rate from: **£100**

The Harbour, Boscastle, Cornwall, PL35 0AQ.
T: 01840 250202

www.wellingtonhotelboscastle.com

- Wellington Hotel, Boscastle
- @thewelly

125
St Moritz Hotel

'Honest, technical cooking' is how new head chef David Williams describes his fare at this popular hotel on the north Cornish coast.

As much a dining destination for locals as a restaurant to feed the hotel's residents, the rather glamorous, contemporary setting is a great spot for a relaxed lunch or intimate dinner. Watch David and team in the open plan kitchen creating dishes such as the squid ink spaghetti fruit de mer dish that's stuffed with tiger prawns, clams, mussels, crab and oysters.

Chef: **David Williams**. 3 course lunch from: **£25**. 3 course dinner from: **£35**. Seats: **70**. Bedrooms: **52**. Room rate from: **£120**

Trebetherick, Wadebridge, Cornwall, PL27 6SD.

T: 01208 862242

www.stmoritzhotel.co.uk

- St Moritz Hotel Cornwall
- @stmoritzhotel
- @stmoritzhotel

126
The Mariners Public House

Set on two levels, with a great people-watching terrace out front, The Mariners is at the heart of unceasingly trendy Rock. As a partnership between Cornwall's über chef Nathan Outlaw and Sharp's Brewery, this is a happy pairing of carefully executed pub food and an array of skilfully brewed beers. Quality is evident throughout, for example, beef is sourced from native breeds at South West farms, dry aged and cooked over coals. Alongside the Sharp's line-up there's always a showcase of beers from select breweries to sip as you enjoy views over the Camel Estuary.

Chef: **Zack Hawke**. 3 course lunch from: **£20**. 3 course dinner from: **£20**. Seats: **100**.

Slipway, Rock, Wadebridge, Cornwall, PL27 6LD.

T: 01208 863679

www.marinersrock.com

- The Mariners, Rock
- @themarinersrock
- @themarinersrock

127
Trevalsa Court Hotel and Restaurant

Simply stylish, this small hotel and restaurant on the cliffs just above the fishing village of Mevagissey has a confident charm. Beautifully decorated and very comfortable, it's not flashy, just quietly lovely with seductive views and a garden to match.

Feast on chef Adam Cawood's accomplished two AA rosette dishes such as stone bass, lobster tortellini, shellfish and chervil bisque with spring onion and rainbow chard in spring, or the rich flavours of duck breast, blackberries, sweet potato, caramelised fennel and celeriac in autumn.

Chef: **Adam Cawood**. 3 course lunch from: **£19.50**. 3 course dinner from: **£25**. Seats: **26.** Bedrooms: **14**. Room rate from: **£120**

School Hill, Mevagissey, Cornwall, PL26 6TH.

T: 01726 842468

www.trevalsa-hotel.co.uk

- Trevalsa Court Hotel and Restaurant
- @trevalsacourt

128
Fistral Beach Hotel and Spa

Expect coastal chic by the bucketload at this hotel with its spacious restaurant overlooking one of Cornwall's premier surfing beaches. The vibrant menu features fresh local seafood, succulent steaks and homemade pasta, with an award winning wine list and relaxed beachside vibe. After dinner enjoy a cocktail in the bar, or at the weekends order a bloody mary with brunch from 8am to 11.30am.

3 course lunch from: **£25**. 3 course dinner from: **£29**. Seats: **150**. Bedrooms: **71**. Room rate from: **£100**

Esplanade Road, Newquay, Cornwall, TR7 1PT.

T: 01637 852221

www.fistralbeachhotel.co.uk

- Fistral Beach Hotel
- @fistralbeachh
- @fistralbeachhotel

INTEGRITY PASSION AUTHENTICITY

The South West's must-have food and drink guides

GET THE GUIDES AT THE BEST RESTAURANTS, HOTELS AND SPECIALITY COFFEE SHOPS, OR ONLINE AT WWW.FOOD-MAG.CO.UK/SHOP

www.saltmedia.co.uk
www.food-mag.co.uk
www.indycoffee.guide

129 Quies Restaurant at Treglos Hotel

TRENCHERMAN'S AWARDS
BEST FRONT OF HOUSE TEAM
2016

ESCAPE TO THE COAST NEAR PADSTOW

It seems only right that the restaurant at Treglos Hotel is named after a cluster of rocks which can be seen jutting out of the ocean just off the shore at Constantine Bay.

The sea and surrounding Cornish landscape feature strongly in chef Gavin Hills' menus, where you can sample delights like Cornish cider cured sea trout or slow braised lamb shoulder croustillant.

In the care of the same family for nearly 50 years, Treglos has a welcoming atmosphere, and no surprise it's recently been notching up the awards. Alongside the usual hotel treats, there's a great spa and an 18 hole golf course to keep you entertained.

Chef: **Gavin Hill**
3 course dinner from: **£36**
Seats: **80**
Bedrooms: **42**
Room rate from: **£135**

Beach Road, Constantine Bay, Padstow, Cornwall, PL28 8JH.
T: 01841 520727

www.treglos**hotel.com**

Treglos Hotel   @tregloshotel   @tregloshotel

The Green Room No. 104

130
Rose in Vale Country House Hotel

Set in an idyllic Cornish valley, complete with babbling brook and a canopy of trees, this country house retreat is a place to grab some time for yourself – along with any lucky chums – and unwind. The two AA rosette Dining Room restaurant is led by chef Tom Bennetts, whose local boy roots and links with surrounding producers means you're in safe hands. The refurbished restaurant has lovely garden views and afterwards you can relax on one of the comfy sofas and indulge in the garden views.

Chef: **Tom Bennetts**. 3 course lunch from: **£24.95**. 3 course dinner from: **£30**. Seats: **80**. Bedrooms: **23**. Room rate from: **£100**

Mithian, St Agnes, Cornwall, TR5 0QD.
T: 01872 552700

www.roseinvalehotel.co.uk

- Rose in Vale Country House Hotel in Cornwall
- @roseinvale
- @roseinvale

131
The Watch House

You'll find The Watch House just by the harbour wall in the centre of stunning St Mawes. A former customs and excise house, then later a pilchard press, it's no-nonsense functional past is echoed in the white walled, simply furnished interior. Split over two floors, with cosy dining booth seating downstairs and jaw-dropping views across the harbour upstairs, it's a relaxed and comfortable place to enjoy lunch or dinner. Chef owner Will Gould makes full use of the dayboat fish and local produce in his appealing menus. You can also grab fish and chips and other delectable takeaway offerings from the outside hatch, the Watch Out.

Chef: **Will Gould**. 3 course lunch from: **£25**. 3 course dinner from: **£35**. Seats: **65**

1 The Square, St Mawes, Cornwall, TR2 5DJ.
T: 01326 270038

www.watchhousestmawes.co.uk

- The Watch House
- @the_watch_house

132
Oliver's

Seasonality, sustainability and local sourcing feature high on the menu at Oliver's. Working closely with his artisan producers, small independents and foragers, chef Ken Symons conjures up bold and exciting menus which are in tune with the seasons, earning the restaurant two AA rosettes, and *Cornwall Life* magazine's Restaurant of the Year 2015.

Husband and wife team Ken and Wendy Symons offer a warm welcome and invite diners to take a seat, relax and enjoy their hospitality.

Chef: **Ken Symons**. 3 course lunch from: **£21.50**. 3 course dinner from: **£25**. Seats: **28**.

33 High Street, Falmouth, Cornwall, TR11 2AD.
T: 01326 218138

www.oliversfalmouth.com

133
Samphire Bistro

A simple philosophy embracing fresh produce, French bistro style cookery and personable service from chef patron Dave Trewin and his team makes dining at Samphire Bistro a real pleasure. With an enviable position close to Falmouth's bustling harbour, the petit eatery makes a great stop for lunch in summer and intimate dinners in winter. Imaginative menus that include Asian and Mediterranean influences offer a real insight into Dave's skills, and you can plump for delicious local fish dishes and sophisticated steaks on more informal occasions.

Chef: **Dave Trewin**. 3 course lunch from: **£15**. 3 course dinner from: **£25**. Seats: **50**

36 Arwenack Street, Falmouth, Cornwall, TR11 3JF.
T: 01326 210759

www.samphire-falmouth.co.uk

- Samphire Restaurant
- @samphirefal

134
Rick Stein's Fish

Happily, the Stein collection has spread its wings to some of the most lovely spots in the South West, including this, its seafood restaurant in Falmouth.

Serving Rick's favourite dishes such as Amritsari fish, Cornish chilli crab and meen kulambu (a fragrant curry from south India), in addition to cracking fish and chips, this contemporary, smart dining destination delivers on its promise.

Chef: **Dominic Gill**. 3 course lunch from: **£16.45**. 3 course dinner from: **£28.28**. Seats: **70**.

Discovery Quay, Falmouth, Cornwall, TR11 3XA.

T: 01326 330050

www.rickstein.com

- Rick Stein's Fish, Falmouth
- @steinsfalmouth
- @theseafood

135
The Ferryboat Inn

Overlooking the Helford river, this 300-year-old pub has a laid-back and friendly atmosphere. Everyone's welcome, including kids and four legged friends. Sit on the terrace or get cosy inside by the open fire and enjoy food prepared by head chef Robert Bunny. With his well rounded menu of British dishes it's clear this chef cares passionately about his farm-to-fork food philosophy. He doesn't have to go far for the freshest fish straight from the boat, or the pub's own oyster farm which you can see outside the window.

Chef: **Robert Bunny**. 3 course lunch or dinner menu from: **£25**. Seats: **60**

Helford Passage, near Falmouth, Cornwall, TR11 5LB.

T: 01326 250625

www.thewrightbrothers.co.uk

- The Ferryboat Inn

136 ⓢ
The Bay Hotel

Just a short hop from the beach up through the garden, The Bay Hotel is in the village of Coverack on Cornwall's famous Lizard Peninsula.

It's light and airy inside, with plenty of big windows through which to enjoy the dramatic coastal views. A daily changing menu makes full use of Cornish produce, including superb seafood which is landed by local dayboats, and the lobsters are a big favourite.

Chef: **Chris Conboye**. Lunch plates from: **£6.95**. 3 course dinner from: **£34.95**. Seats: **36**. Bedrooms: **14**. Room rate from: **£120**

North Corner, Coverack, Helston, Cornwall, TR12 6TF.

T: 01326 280464

www.thebayhotel.co.uk

- The Bay Hotel Coverack
- @bayhotelc
- @coverackbay

137
Alba

Housed in a former lifeboat house, chef patron Grant Nethercott's "natural and eclectic" approach to cookery is echoed in the restaurant's eye-catching combination of cool Cornish design and quirky original artwork.

Chill out over cocktails and small plates at the street level bar, or dine on the first floor for Grant's award winning, French-British fusion food with panoramic views of St Ives harbour. With a couple of glasses of crisp white and an impressive range of fresh seafood dishes, you'd be hard pressed to find a better spot in which to while away a few hours.

Chef: **Grant Nethercott**. 3 course lunch from: **£25**. 3 course dinner from: **£33**. Seats: **37**

Old Lifeboat House, Wharf Road, St Ives, Cornwall, TR26 1LF.

T: 01736 797222

www.alba-stives.co.uk

- Alba Restaurant and Bar St.Ives
- @albarestaurant
- @alba_stives

138
Tolcarne Inn

You can't get a restaurant much closer to its suppliers than the Tolcarne Inn.

This 18th century pub is a stone's throw from Newlyn fish market, arguably one of the best and most diverse in the country, so there are rich pickings to be had for Tolcarne's chef owner Ben Tunnicliffe. This talented chef deservedly has a loyal following, which comes as no surprise on tasting the well put together and simple dishes he creates from those spankingly fresh ingredients.

Chef: **Ben Tunnicliffe**. 3 course lunch from: **£22.50**. 3 course dinner from: **£27.75**. Seats: **50**

Tolcarne Place, Newlyn, Penzance, Cornwall, TR18 5PR.

T: **01736 363074**

www.tolcarneinn.co.uk

- Tolcarne Inn
- @ben_tunnicliffe

139
2 Fore Street Restaurant

Head to Mousehole, one of the most picturesque harbours in Cornwall, to discover this popular bistro. Call in for brunch, lunch and dinner and choose between dining inside with views of Mounts Bay or eating alfresco in the pretty courtyard garden. Local seafood dishes like the Newlyn crab double baked souffle or shell roasted scallops with garlic and herbs, come courtesy of chef Joe Wardell who trained under Raymond Blanc.

Chef: **Joe Wardell**. 3 course lunch from: **£20**. 3 course dinner from: **£28**. Seats: **36**

2 Fore Street, Mousehole, Penzance, Cornwall, TR19 6PF.

T: **01736 731164**

www.2forestreet.co.uk

INSIDER'S TIP

'I'm looking forward to visiting Jude Kereama at Kota (No. 115) as I ate there about six years ago and had a fantastic meal. It's one of the best located restaurants in the country, with cooking to match.'

Nick Evans, head chef, St Petroc's Bistro **No. 101**

Restaurant	N°	Restaurant	N°
2 Fore Street Restaurant	139	The Green Room	104
ABode Exeter	59	The Grill Room	89
The Acorn Inn	48	Halsetown Inn	117
Alba	137	Harris's Restaurant	122
The Arundell Arms Hotel and Restaurant	62	The Hartnoll Hotel	75
Asquiths Restaurant	96	Harvey Nichols Second Floor Restaurant	19
Augustus	38	HIX Oyster and Fish House	46
Barbican Kitchen	85	The Horn of Plenty	64
The Bath Priory	21	The Horse	82
The Bay at Hotel Penzance	121	Hotel Endsleigh	63
The Bay Hotel	136	Howard's House	10
The Bear and Swan	32	The Idle Rocks	110
The Bell at Ramsbury	6	Ilsington Country House Hotel and Spa	83
Ben's Cornish Kitchen	120	Jamie Oliver's Fifteen Cornwall	105
Best Western The Grange at Oborne	44	The Kensington Arms	28
Boringdon Hall	87	Kota	115
Captain's Club Hotel and Spa	51	Langdon Court Restaurant	86
The Carlyon Bay Hotel	97	Langmans Restaurant	93
Cary Arms	73	The Lazy Toad Inn	76
Casamia	20	Lewtrenchard Manor	61
The Castle Inn Hotel	13	Little Barwick House	37
The Cedar Restaurant	35	The Longs Arms	16
The Chequers	23	Lucknam Park Hotel and Spa	8
The Coach House by Michael Caines	54	Lumière	3
Combe Grove	31	The Mariners Public House	126
The Cornish Arms (St Merryn)	103	The Marlborough Tavern	22
The Cornish Arms (Tavistock)	84	The Masons Arms	55
Crab House Cafe	47	Menu Gordon Jones	25
Dartington Hall	91	The Methuen Arms	9
The (Exmoor) Beastro	74	The Millbrook Inn	88
The Ferryboat Inn	135	The Miners Country Inn	4
Fistral Beach Hotel and Spa	128	The Mint Room - Bath	30
The Fontmell	49	The Mint Room - Bristol	29
The Fox	17	The Muddy Duck	15
The Galley Restaurant	79	Mullion Cove Hotel	113
Gidleigh Park	60	The NoBody Inn	81
Glazebrook House Hotel	71	The Northey Arms	14
The Globe	42	The Old House at Home	12
Goodfellows Restaurant	33	The Olive Tree	24
The Greedy Goose	68	Oliver's	132

INDEX

Restaurant	N°
The Orange Tree Restaurant	92
Outlaw's Fish Kitchen	99
The Pear Tree at Purton	7
Pendennis Restaurant at The Royal Duchy Hotel	112
The Pilgrims Restaurant	34
Plantation House Hotel and Restaurant	70
The Pony & Trap	27
Porthminster Beach Cafe	118
Prince Hall Hotel and Restaurant	66
Psalter's Restaurant at The Luttrell Arms	40
Q Restaurant at the Old Quay House Hotel	95
The Quarterdeck at The Nare	109
The Queens Arms	36
Quies Restaurant at Treglos Hotel	129
The Restaurant @ Centurion	39
Restaurant Nathan Outlaw	98
Rick Stein, Porthleven	114
Rick Stein's Cafe	102
Rick Stein's Fish	134
The Rising Sun Inn	41
Riverside Restaurant	43
The Riviera Hotel and Restaurant	58
Rock Salt Cafe	67
Rodean Restaurant	80
Rose in Vale Country House Hotel	130
Roswarne Manor Restaurant	116
Royal Seven Stars Hotel	90
The Rusty Bike	77
Saffron	107
The Salty Monk Restaurant with Rooms	57
The Salutation Inn	78
Samphire Bistro	133
Saunton Sands Hotel	52
The Seafood Restaurant	100
The Slaughters Country Inn	2
The Slaughters Manor House	1
Soar Mill Cove Hotel and Spa	72
The Springer Spaniel	123
St Moritz Hotel	125
St Petroc's Bistro	101

Restaurant	N°
The Swan	56
Tabb's Restaurant	108
Talland Bay Hotel	94
Three Daggers	18
The Three Lions	45
Three Tuns Freehouse	11
Tolcarne Inn	138
The Treby Arms	69
Trevalsa Court Hotel and Restaurant	127
Two Bridges Hotel	65
The Victoria Inn	119
The Watch House	131
The Water's Edge	111
Watersmeet Hotel	53
The Wellington Hotel	124
WestBeach	50
The Wheatsheaf Combe Hay	26
Wild Garlic Restaurant	5
Zacry's at Watergate Bay Hotel	106